It's a
LOVE
STORY

"Lincee Ray is one of my very favorite people because she is hilarious, kind, honest, and full of heart. And, lucky for you, every one of those qualities shines in the pages of her new book, *It's a Love Story*. Her words will make you laugh out loud, wipe away a few tears, and think back to what your own love stories have meant in your life. Most of all, you will fall in love with Lincee because she is a delight in every way! This book is a must-read, can't miss, good time from cover to cover! I'd give it my final rose every time."

Melanie Shankle, *New York Times* bestselling author
of *Church of the Small Things*

"*It's a Love Story* is vintage Lincee Ray: tender, nostalgic, self-deprecating, funny, and, in all the best ways, a little bit snarky. This book is a delight to read, to savor—and it will spur you on to some serious gratitude as you remember and reflect on the loves of your own life: the four-legged ones, the familial ones, the pop culture ones, the long-lasting ones, the life-giving ones, and the eternal One. You'll laugh, you'll cry, and you'll want to watch *Clueless* all over again. It's a win all the way around. I loved it!"

Sophie Hudson, author of *Giddy Up, Eunice*
and cohost of *The Big Boo Cast*

"Everyone loves a good love story, and in Lincee's book, she covers every type of love story you can possibly imagine. Lincee's storytelling ability brings you in like a best friend offering you a cup of tea and a seat on the sofa. You want to sit with her for hours and just listen. Get your drink of choice, plop yourself down on your sofa, and spend some time with Lincee. You won't regret it!"

Jamie Ivey, bestselling author of *If You Only Knew*
and host of *The Happy Hour with Jamie Ivey* podcast

"Lincee Ray is one of the funniest, most relatable writers out there today. *It's a Love Story* will have you nodding and laughing and wishing that Lincee were your next-door neighbor."

Jennifer Fulwiler, SiriusXM radio host
and author of *One Beautiful Dream*

It's a LOVE STORY

From Happily to Ever After

Lincee Ray

Revell

a division of Baker Publishing Group
Grand Rapids, Michigan

Published by Revell
a division of Baker Publishing Group
PO Box 6287, Grand Rapids, MI 49516-6287
www.revellbooks.com

Printed in the United States of America

Library of Congress Cataloging-in-Publication Data
Names: Ray, Lincee, 1975– author.
Title: It's a love story : from happily to ever after / Lincee Ray.
Description: Grand Rapids, MI : Revell, [2019]
Identifiers: LCCN 2018049154 | ISBN 9780800728465 (pbk.)
Subjects: LCSH: Ray, Lincee, 1975– | Christian women—Conduct of life. | Love. | Christian life—United States.
Classification: LCC BV4527 .R3849 2018 | DDC 248.8/43—dc23
LC record available at https://lccn.loc.gov/2018049154

The Author is represented by Alive Literary Agency, 7680 Goddard Street, Suite 200, Colorado Springs, Colorado 80920, www.aliveliterary.com.

19 20 21 22 23 24 25   7 6 5 4 3 2 1

For Daddy—I love you

Disclaimer

I share some rather embarrassing stuff in this book. Of course, I have changed the names because I would be mortified if any of these people knew what young, impressionable Lincee was thinking. *Can you die from hives?* My throat is thick just thinking about it, but I trust it will all be worth it if I can make you laugh and feel less losery about yourself.

Suffering for our craft is what we creative types do.

Now, if you're from Hallsville, Texas, try to be cool about certain details you're about to read. Don't try to puzzle any of the pieces together to figure out who I'm talking about. Just know that if the description sounds like someone who was in your physics class with Mr. Strickland or that guy who looked really good in his football jersey or the girl who was a class officer or the person who epitomized what it meant to be the most popular kid in school, it's not who you think it is and you should just move on to the next chapter.

If you ignore the request above and you do want to venture a guess, don't message me and ask me if you are correct. You don't want me to die from hives, do you?

Contents

Contents

Introduction

That's the story of, that's the glory of LOVE

I remember the first time I fell in love. His name was Logan, and he was super dreamy with sandy-blond hair and crystal-blue eyes. His family had moved from Kentucky, so his accent was Southern. Logan was smart, charming, and athletic, and I looked forward to spending time with him.

Logan was also a fictional character in The Baby-Sitters Club book series.

Bring on the judgment. I can handle it. I was a bibliophile with an active imagination, and I let it soar. I crushed hard when my boy showed up in book number ten, titled *Logan Likes Mary Anne!* and I don't believe it's one bit bizarre for a young girl approaching adolescence to imagine herself with a fake boyfriend.

You want bizarre? I was jealous of Mary Anne. That's bizarre. And here's another alarming fact: I didn't have to Google the book title of Logan's Baby-Sitters Club debut before I typed it. I can't remember why I walked into my bathroom three minutes ago, but I can pull thirty-year-old useless information from the recesses of my mind without even trying.

In short, Logan made an impact on my tender heart.

Why did he give me a squishy feeling on my insides? Was there a real Logan out there for me? Did I have a shot with him if I acted exactly like Mary Anne? And who taught me how to fall in love in the first place?

Walt Disney, of course.

Uncle Walt has been a signature staple in my life from the very beginning. My love of books came from his fairy tales. My love of Mickey Mouse came from his imagination. Without a doubt, my idea of true love came from his animated princess movies.

I figured I could take a job in the forest and be a maid for a bunch of dwarves. They could mine gemstones while I bided my time waiting for the prince.

How am I biding my time? Well, there was this apple-biting, sleeping-curse situation, and I've ended up in a coffin, but it's cool. I'll wake up when my prince finds me and kisses me so we can go ahead and start living our happily ever after.

I do appreciate it when a man pursues me.

I believe our obsession with love, love stories, romance, and relationships plays a big part in our own stories, for better or for worse. As we get older, we realize love is more than the romantic happily ever after. Love is bigger and broader and much better than that.

My mama loves Hawaii, thanks to Elvis Presley. Daddy is happiest when he's burning something. My friend Lara's closet is one-third maroon-colored clothing because she loves the Texas A&M Aggies. I often wonder if my sister would save me first or her pug from a burning building.

When we say "I love Dr Pepper," that really and truly is part of our love story as human beings who were made in the image of God. Because those feelings of love—for people or places or things—all reflect the very essence of who He is. The squishy feeling is for Him. I believe we were created with this specific longing ingrained in our souls that can be fulfilled only by the One who loves us most. I wrote this book to encourage anyone reading to recognize that feeling. Although we'll never be wholly fulfilled this side of heaven, love lives in our hearts and souls to remind us that day is coming.

And it will be glorious.

This book is for the people who tear up when John Legend's "All of Me" is the background track for any movie. It's for everyone who's embarrassed to divulge how many times they've visited Disney World as an adult. It's for those who feel a twinge of nostalgia when they think of their youth or feel deeply humbled when someone in need whispers a grateful *thank you*.

This book is for the dog lover, the Broadway baby, the foodie, and the musician. It's for the girl who was crushed by that boy in high school or the wise individual who lives for Little Debbie Oatmeal Creme Pies. This person reveres the Dread Pirate Roberts, the people from Africa, Michael Jackson, and swing dancing.

The love stories you're about to read have made up the tapestry of my life. I hope you can see pieces of your own story in them and find comfort that you weren't the only one obsessed with New Kids on the Block as a collective unit. (FYI: The song "Please Don't Go Girl" is all about me. Deal with it.)

A quick note to those who happened to pick up this book and immediately rolled their eyes at the thought of a girl begging a guy with some form of "Pick me, choose me, love me." I have news for you, dear friend.

The love story is here to stay. That's why forty-seven million individuals got up at the crack of dawn to watch a bunch of fancy people in eccentric hats and dapper suits file into St. George's Chapel to witness the royal wedding of a ginger prince to an American actress on a basic cable network.

It's time to get on board.

1

Fur and Feathers

For those of us who LOVE *four-legged friends*
alongside the human children on our Christmas cards

My first love story includes a stack of books from the library and a doll. *Anne of Green Gables* and Strawberry Shortcake never let me down. Around this time, though, I also developed an ardent love for animals. Kudos to me for filling my emotional bucket with something that can love me back, am I right?

But there was one exception: Mama's poodle, named Babette.

Yes, that fact contradicts my aforementioned ardent love for animals, so I should warn you that this love is strong and reciprocated only about half the time.

Babette was pretentious and too dainty for my pet needs. I required something adorable, white, and furry. What I got was a Shetland pony named Trixie.

Now, I can acknowledge Trixie as a legitimate pet and appreciate my father procuring for me an animal so many children long for in the months leading up to their birthdays. The problem? I wasn't one of those children. Neither was my sister. I wanted a cute puppy to push around in my doll carriage. I tried with all my might to befriend the pony. I fed her carrots and tried to braid her mane. Sadly, Trixie didn't like to be ridden or walked around or petted. I'm saying she was a large version of Babette.

One day I decided to put a saddle on Trixie and ride her out to the pond. She was being a bit ornery when I hopped up onto her back, and with the first nudge of my heels, she took off as though she were a contender for the Preakness. My lethargic pony, who previously had little to no desire to move, had blown past trot and was full-on galloping toward my father, who couldn't hear me because he was mowing the pasture.

My life flashed before my eyes. I saw Logan, Strawberry Shortcake, and Anne bid me farewell as if they knew what was coming next. Before I could brace myself, Trixie bucked me off. As I went sailing through the air, my sweet mother rushed over to catch her daughter. I landed in a heap at her feet, but I gave her a solid E for effort.

After the Trixie incident, we switched back to canines.

My People Are Dog People

We had sixteen different dogs while I was growing up. I know that sounds ludicrous, but my family made a list of their names one Easter, and that's how I know. I played hard with some, dressed the smaller puppies in Cabbage Patch Kids clothes, and loved each one with all my heart.

Except Babette.

The first day of second grade proved to be a pivotal time in both my real education and family pet education. I was in the Red Hot reading group, and I felt pretty good about how I'd flown through my summer book list. As the big yellow bus rolled up to the end of our driveway, I stood confident, looking forward to being an upperclassman on the Hallsville elementary school campus.

I climbed the steps, found my seat, waved to my dad from the window, and watched the bus run over our dog Buford.

I'm so sorry to bum you out. You read that correctly. I chose to spare you the gory details, but suffice it to say, it was a traumatic event for any second grader to witness.

I approached family pets differently after that day. My mind warned me not to become attached, but my heart ditched that brazen thought with the first whiff of puppy breath.

Oh, the puppies. So many of them. All the time. That's what happens when you grow up on a significant piece of land out in the country. Our two German shepherds named CK and Sara were rock star dogs. CK was the male, named after Daddy's restaurant, Catfish King, and Sara would sit by the stereo speakers and tilt her head whenever the song "Sara" by Starship came on the radio.

She was a dog genius, and way into '80s hair bands, like me. How could I not love her?

In my adolescent brain, Sara and CK loved each other very much. You can imagine Little Lincee's joy when Sara gave birth to ten puppies in her first litter. I named them all, and I tied colorful bows around each neck so we could tell them apart.

Mama drew the short stick and had to explain to me that we couldn't keep them all. In her defense, ten is a lot to handle when dog breeding isn't your first, second, or third line of work. But still, the reality that I wouldn't see these little guys grow up dampened my every waking moment. My parents tried to make me feel better by reminding me that our dogs were going to a good home.

You're picturing a rough-and-tumble little boy with a backward baseball cap and dirty face hugging sweet little Gomer with the blue ribbon around his neck, aren't you? Or maybe a shy little girl smiling as squatty Pippy with the purple ribbon flops in her direction, slipping on the hardwood floor with her soft puppy feet. What about the old, old man who lost his wife last year and his children and grandchildren pooled all their money to buy the runt of the litter, Boomer, to be Granddaddy's new companion?

Nope. The Ray German shepherds were headed to the Harrison County Sheriff's Department so they could train to be drug dogs.

Drug dogs. My beloved Sweetie and Heinz in their pink and rainbow ribbons would be sniffing out crack cocaine from common criminals and street youths for a living.

After my four-legged relatives left me to help kids say nope to dope, I kept a safe distance from the family pets. It's a good thing, too, because very few of our pets died of natural causes. Again, life in the country can be tricky.

Gizmo was our teeny-tiny yippy dog, which meant he not only was mobile and easily placed inside a doll carriage, but he didn't mind wearing hair clips. He was the first to reach an age when a decision had to be made to put him out of his misery because his quality of life was stretched so thin it was about to snap. That opened an untapped realm of sadness.

Here's another thing country folks do: we bury our animals in the backyard. Way over in one corner of my parents' property is a pet cemetery with all our dogs' collars buckled into the chain-link fence. It's a lovely reminder of their time here on earth with us, as well as a reality check for all the pets who have come and gone in the past three decades.

I never thought this was peculiar until last year. My niece has experienced one or two family pet deaths, and she understands our little cemetery back behind Daddy's barn. Addison picks flowers and lays them on the ground every now and again. We all think it's sweet. But when she asked me if we were going to bury my grandmother Mimi in the yard with Chewy and Creede, I gleaned that it was time to supplement our country way of living with tales from the big city.

I Held a Cat by Its Tail Once—Just Once

I've been asked on more than one occasion why I don't have a pet since most single people do. I smile and make up stories about how I travel all the time and would never want to board a dog, or how I feel guilty that the dog wouldn't have a yard to run around and play ball in.

Lies. All lies. I don't have a pet to call my own because I can't handle the reality that my dog's collar will one day be affixed to that chain-link fence out back. When Buford died that fateful first-day-of-school morning, I experienced sadness like never before. When we made the decision to have Gizmo put to sleep, I was riddled with guilt and fought tears for months. With each German shepherd—those powerful narc dogs—that walked away with a police officer, a little piece of my heart went too.

Notice exactly zero of my personal pet stories involve felines. Give me a cat, and I swear to you I'll morph into the eccentric spinster at the end of the street. The next thing I know, my house will be the one you won't let your kids go to for trick-or-treating anymore, because that one time there was a fur ball stuck to a half-wrapped lemon saltwater taffy.

Look, I love cats.

The musical. I love *Cats* the musical. I have a considerable aversion to real ones.

This dislike was probably born out of medical necessity. You see, I'm allergic to cats. If I sit on a couch a cat has been on or near, my eyes become a watery, itchy mess and my air passages start to close.

Plus, most cats seem a bit snobby to me. That's my opinion, but it's still true.

The irony of it all is that I attract cats. I have friends who never see their cats until I come over. Then they sit directly on my lap and stare at me as though I'm invading their personal space.

I've been on the receiving end of a courtship with a cat named Drake. He was the resident apartment building cat named after the street where we lived. No one claimed him, but he considered the complex his home. He would sit outside my window and meow for hours. I had to turn up my TV volume to properly ignore him. Then Drake took matters into his own paws and decided to profess his love through a grand gesture.

Let's begin with the headless lizard. Sure, it was only the size of my finger, but nonetheless, it was both dead and without its head. It took a lot of courage for me to pick up the corner of my favorite Christmas doormat, showcasing whimsical nutcrackers, and fling the reptile into a nearby bush.

A few days later, Drake left me a mostly dead frog. That poor chubby thing probably never saw Drake coming. It took a little more chutzpah to fling its carcass into the bush.

But one day still torments me. It will forever be the reason I will never, ever fly out my front door in a rush without looking below to see what treats may have been bestowed upon me.

Winter isn't much more than a blip on the radar in my part of Texas, but when I opened the door, I felt a gush of cold air. I ran to find my gloves, and in my haste to get to work, I flung the door open again and started to step out to greet my day with a positive attitude. Praise be to the good Lord, I happened to look down.

It was like a St. Valentine's Day massacre.

I was in mid-step, and it took all the strength in my legs to catapult myself over the grisly mess. I turned around to find a headless rat. And, dear reader, when I say rat, I mean r-a-t. We're talking Charlotte's Templeton on vacation at the county fair. By the look of things, it had given Drake the fight of his life. Blood was splattered on my door, my window, and the carcass bush.

I started to sick myself out looking at the remains of this rodent. And that's when I noticed one of my gloves was among the perished.

I guess in my attempt to hoist myself up and over, I had lost my grip on one glove and it landed in the middle of the aftermath. I loved those gloves.

Notice I said *loved.*

Even being used to dismantled frogs and lizards, I had to give myself a major pep talk just to try to strategically lean over far enough to lock my door. And all the free puppies in the world couldn't summon the courage it would take me to fling any entrails into the carcass bush. I somehow managed to lock the door and then run as if the mangled rat could chase me. I spotted Drake and yelled "Bad kitty!" as I sprinted for my life—with one cold hand.

Later I called the apartment people and told them a small horse had been murdered on my front porch and that someone needed to make sure it wasn't there when I returned home. I encouraged the guy to bring bleach as well.

"That cat must really love you," he said. "It's a sign of affection when they leave something like that at your door. It's like a peace offering."

Maybe a nice gift basket full of wine and cheese next time?

One weekend, a new neighbor moved in with her outdoor/indoor cat named Fifi. Later that week, I heard a noise that made me jump out of my skin. I ran to the window with my phone in my hand, ready to call nine-one-one to report a stabbing.

Drake and Fifi were fighting, and Fifi was the instigator! They were making the most awful noise you've ever heard in your life. I had to go out and break up the altercation. Drake, being a gentleman cat, wasn't going to get into it full-on with a girl feline. Fifi ran off. Drake went to sulk by the pool.

That night, Drake was sprawled by my door where my mat used to be. Feeling sorry for him, I scratched him three times with the tip of my shoe. Just three.

The next morning, I found a headless bird beside the carcass bush.

Bye-Bye Blackbird

We've clearly established that cats adore me, and that I in turn enjoy them from a distance on most occasions. Other creatures that find me nonthreatening include mosquitos.

And woodpeckers.

Why is my example so specific to one species of bird? Am I an ornithological weirdo?

Perhaps. I did collect feathers as a child . . . until Mama told me I'd get mites.

My example is so specific because I had a personal experience with a woodpecker once. I remember it as though it were ten years ago, which it was.

I was asleep at my parents' house when I was abruptly jolted from my slumber by a woodpecker pecking on the bedroom windowpane. Obviously, this is unacceptable behavior, so I banged on the pane to make him stop, which he did.

The next morning, Woody's pecks returned, only this time they seemed distant and somewhat muffled. I searched and searched, and then finally discovered the bird had managed to magic his way into the attic where he was building a lovely summer home.

Mama was both calm and irrational at the news. She had no problem crawling up into the attic to shoo a rogue woodpecker, and her peaceful state of mind baffled me. On the other hand, the idea of Woody crapping all over her graduation announcements from 1964 annoyed her to no end.

When we have critters to catch, we Rays do what we have to do, at least in most cases. Mama asked me to fetch the swimming pool skimmer net thing. Its traditional purpose is to scoop up leaves from the deep end. Today it would scoop up a live bird. (The net has come in handy in multiple emergency situations.)

Mama pulled the string that lowers the folded stairs that go up to the attic. The springs creaked as she clambered up into the abyss, making her way through boxes of my childhood memorabilia and every floral comforter and brightly colored duvet we've owned since we moved into the house in 1980. She effortlessly caught Woody as my head cheered from the opening in the floor. Mama released Woody outside, into the wild, and I praised her for being so brave.

Hours later, I heard Woody continuing his remodeling efforts, flipping our attic into something more amenable to his needs. Mama wasn't so peaceful this go-around. She retrieved the swimming pool net and repeated the same steps from before. This time she walked to the edge of the property and bid Woody adieu.

To her utter frustration, Woody came back for a third round.

Oh, it's on, Woody. Prepare for the Thunderdome. We don't need another hero. You are going down.

Woody's temper had swelled since our last engagement. When we attempted to daintily shove him into the net, he channeled his inner ancestors and dive-bombed us like a pterodactyl. All I could think about was Phoebe from *Friends* shouting, "My eyes! My eyes!" as she witnessed Monica and Chandler making out through the window. (Actually, Phoebe saw them making out up against the window.)

Mama tried to balance on skinny two-by-fours all over the attic floor without falling into the second-story bedrooms. She extended the pole and flailed about, figuratively crossing her fingers that one of these sporadic sweeps would end with a cheeky woodpecker miraculously enclosed in pool equipment.

Unwilling to lose an eye in a heroic bird rescue, I made the brilliant decision to don my hot-pink swimmer's goggles and some denim oven mitts as a precaution. I quickly put on my Bobcat letterman jacket, because, duh, it was hanging right there, and I hoped the worn leather arms hadn't been compromised by decades of stagnant attic heat. I needed the leather arms to guard me from pervasive pecks. And mites.

Mama started spouting unladylike words at both me and the bird, but we finally wrangled Woody into the net as he sat atop a gigantic ice-blue furry bunny my dad won at a fair in 1979. I'm happy to report that no one fell through the floor, and that only one piece of Occupied Japan pottery was destroyed during the emancipation.

Query: What to do with the bird? For some reason, we didn't have a car. I can't remember the specifics, but that's important to note for this next part of the narrative. Because we couldn't physically drive Woody out to the middle of nowhere and set him free far, far away from the house, we stuck him in the barbecue smoker for safekeeping until my dad got back with his truck.

Everyone calm down. You weren't there! You don't know! This made perfect sense to both me and my mother at the time, so we went with it.

Luckily, Daddy came home shortly after and laughed at my goggles and oven mitts, and we all headed to the smoker so he could carry Woody away to harass another family. He opened the smoker lid and we were all shocked.

I know you're thinking Woody left this world because of asphyxiation. Although that is a sad, sad thought, you're terribly wrong. This was the bird with massive determination. He was like the woodpecker version of Lloyd in *Say Anything*, holding up a boombox outside my window playing "In Your Eyes." He was like Romeo calling up to me, Juliet, on my balcony. He had perched before a crazed woman and her daughter, chirping, "Isn't She Lovely" like a feathered Stevie Wonder.

Woody was gone. He wasn't in the smoker, and my father couldn't control his laughter as he spit out, "You didn't consider that the bird would fly out of the smokestack?"

Uh, no we did not.

We all traipsed back into the house, up the stairs, and into the attic, ready to bow down to the great woodpecker. He was there, chilling on a huge stack of important *Southern Living* magazines Mama is still convinced she'll make a vision board with someday. Mama caught Woody easily. It was a fun game to him now. He had no idea a man was about to drive him away to the city limits.

Mama and I watched as Daddy hauled our little almost-a-pet bird down the driveway. I must admit, it was like watching a child go off to college. Woody, Mama, and I had been through so much. He was a good bird. A good, extremely mischievous bird. I hope he found a nice fence post or barn to destroy.

That's what pets will do to a person. They wiggle their way into our lives and create unforgettable stories. They were always happy to see me and let me ride their backs and cuddle with them in the colder months. Memories of Shallie, White Dog, Bubba, and even Woody produce a mental slide show of smiles, giggles, freedom, and joy.

They were part of our family. All of them.

2

Young Love

For those of us who would LOVE to forget our first kiss

As I got older, my focus slowly switched from baby dolls, illusive literary crushes, and furry friends to something with a little more substance: homework.

I'd like to tell you I'm kidding, but I'm not. I was a late bloomer when it came to boys. Not until high school did actual breathing young males with a pulse show up on my radar. That's when I began the search to find my real-life Logan.

Everyone at Hallsville High School had to take a couple of fine arts electives to graduate. Drill team met one of those requirements for me. Theater met the other.

I absolutely excelled in my freshman theater class. I enjoyed prose, poetry, plays, and improv, and I even dabbled in acting in one-act plays. I also crushed my end-of-year project. It was painstakingly planned and exhaustively carried out in just under the five-minute mark. I wish you could see the video, but my words will have to do.

The first thing you need to know is that Disney released the original *Beauty and the Beast* animation on November 22, 1991.

On November 23 of that year, I made it my mission to switch from learning the lyrics of PM Dawn's "Set Adrift on Memory Bliss" to finding, purchasing, listening, and memorizing the *Beauty and the Beast* soundtrack in its entirety.

Fifteen-year-old Lincee was infatuated.

Naturally, I elected to showcase my *Beauty and the Beast* fixation during my theater arts final. I had an entire audience of captive peers. How ideal!

The assignment was simple, with only one rule: Ms. Clark instructed us to blend three different theatrical elements in our piece. For example, you could incorporate set design (#1) and lighting (#2) while reciting a poem (#3).

I went above and beyond. I confiscated my mother's animal-print jumpsuit from the seventies, a purple cape we had in our costume box, my grandmother Mimi's blue apron, and a white shirt from my closet to forge an ensemble that was half beast, half Belle. A killer costume design was element #1.

Next I painted one side of my face like an aggressive cat (makeup = element #2) and borrowed some costume cat paws from a friend. I like to think the fact I had a friend with cat paws was God's way of blessing this moment in my life.

From behind the curtain, I recited (prose = element #3) the opening "once upon a time" monologue into the microphone with great gusto, pausing in places for dramatic effect. Then I played the title soundtrack and lip-synced every word. (Bonus element. *Holla!*)

I chose the human version of the "Beauty and the Beast" duet because it's more intense than the one Mrs. Potts sings. I turned to my Belle side when Celine Dion sang and to my beast side when Peabo Bryson sang, and I faced the audience when they sang in harmony.

Like I said, for all intents and purposes, on a creativity scale of one to ten, I nailed it. Regrettably, the nailing was clouded by an unfavorable incident from earlier in the year. Even Celine and Peabo couldn't assuage the damage. They may have even perpetuated the myth that I was having an allergic reaction to all my feelings.

Earlier that year, I attended my first high school dance. I'm pretty sure ninth graders were forbidden from entering the premises, but since I was someone's date, this unofficial rule didn't apply to me.

That's right. A boy asked me to the dance. And not just any boy. The cutest boy in school. Oh, I haven't even told you the best part yet.

He was a junior. I know.

His name was Miles. And for those of you from the same teeny-tiny town I grew up in, if for one second you think that's his real name, I'd like to bless your heart multiple times and include a condescending head tilt. You'll probably do some sort of outlandish math to try to figure out the given name of said hunk, and I applaud your efforts.

You were a mathlete, weren't you? Quadruple digits on the old SAT score, am I right? Good for you. I hope your career as an accountant or physicist has served you well, smarty-pants.

Here's the deal: I'm about to drop some emotionally raw ambiance on you in a way that surpasses embarrassment by light years. Why should I put the Abercrombie model through the same torture by calling him by his real name? I don't think so. Say hello to Miles.

Miles was a heartthrob. Everyone thought so. Tall, dark, and handsome. He was an athlete who drove a Camaro. Take a moment to swoon at that tidbit of information like I did back in 1991.

Are we all good? Let's continue the story.

Miles asked me to go to the dance with him in the hallway outside of Mrs. Robinson's Spanish class. My best friend, Julie, warned me that I needed to proceed with caution, since this one extracurricular activity could catapult me into the upper echelon of Hallsville High School's social circles. It would all boil down to one weighty decision: wardrobe.

Rumor had it that Miles liked to dance. I heard he even knew how to handle an eight count with a partner. And since I was bound for Broadway in a few years, maybe Miles wanted to enjoy the dance with an actual dancer. My ensemble required specific considerations to get the job done. I also had to convey that the look took little to no effort.

This old thing? Oh, I just threw it on right before I ran out the door. That dense fragrant cloud? Why it's Safari by Ralph Lauren. Thank you for noticing!

Sidebar one: I think it's important to share that I never made it to Broadway, but I'm proud of Young Lincee for holding on to that dream. I also think it's darling that she assumed Miles chose her from a sea of adorable freshman girls because she knew all the choreography from Michael Jackson's "Thriller" video. Keep reaching for the stars, kids!

Sidebar two: The "Thriller" choreography has resurfaced at least three times at two wedding receptions and one high school reunion. Thank you, MTV.

The foundation of my perfect outfit was the Z Cavaricci blue jeans. I thought the limitless pleats promoted optimal give and take for doing the Running Man. I paired the Z's with a simple white shirt that accentuated my waist, a huge pair of silver shrimp earrings, and a few twist-a-beads for a pop of color. My hair was easy. I surmised I would be hot from all the dancing, so I tied a white-and-blue polka-dot ribbon around my ponytail, grabbed my red Liz Claiborne purse, and paid my sister five dollars to drive me to the dance.

I met Miles at the school that Friday night for reasons I don't remember. What I can recall is that my girlfriends and I were all spending the night at Melissa's house, and my parents were aware that Miles would be taking me there after the dance.

For those of you who think this story is going to end with my parents picking me up at the county jail because Miles crashed his car into the Dairy Queen sign on Highway 80 thanks to a little friend I like to call Boone's Farm Strawberry Hill wine, prepare to be disappointed. My friend group followed the rules. So did Miles. *Wah, wah.*

Miles arrived at the school with a pack of guy friends. He wore manly acid-washed denim overalls by Tommy Hilfiger. You may be wondering if my description of the overalls is an overexaggeration because I used the words *manly* and *acid-washed* in the same sentence. I get it, but it's an accurate picture that's seared into my brain. He looked good. Really good.

He sought me out immediately and pulled me onto the dance floor. Lo and behold, the rumors were true. Miles could move. We're talking a little bit of Swayze mixed with a whole lotta MC Hammer.

Lead the way, Twinkle Toes.

That year, 1991, was a banner year for dance music. Miles and I dominated any C+C Music Factory song that found its way into the rotation. EMF's "Unbelievable" was apropos, thanks to our commitment to fancy footwork. How we managed to have serious fun dancing to Michael Bolton's "Time, Love and Tenderness" remains a mystery. I adore Lord Bolton, but the idea that we got our groove on to that song proves we were working at 100 percent.

Let's not dismiss the power of the cool R&B hit, either. Everything Bryan Adams did, he did it for me. The band Damn Yankees took us high enough. We visited the refreshment table during "I Adore Mi Amor." That Color Me Badd single ruled the radio, and anyone with ears was sick of it. Finally, Timmy T's "One More Try" brought the house down in a totally chill-to-the-max sort of way. To this day, it still holds a special place in my heart.

The peak of the night had to be the moment an actual circle formed around us while we hip-hopped to "Good Vibrations" by

Marky Mark and the Funky Bunch. The crowd started chanting, "Go, Lincee! Go, Miles! Go, Lincee! Go, Miles!"

Listen up, people. This is how legends are made. I'm sure my classmates talked about our skills for years. They probably had to retire that song from all future soirees in the cafetorium.

Okay, the circle could have been a complete figment of my active imagination, and maybe I morphed my growing crush on this boy into an actual hallucination. Either way, I had the time of my life. I'd also like to report that my Z Cavariccis did not let me down.

On the way home from the dance, Miles put a cassette in the tape deck of his Camaro. As I live and breathe it was the *Beaches* soundtrack. I felt both excited and fearful.

A) This dude owns the *Beaches* soundtrack = woo-hoo!

B) If he plays "Wind Beneath My Wings" I will tuck and roll right out of this dope car onto the pavement and walk to Melissa's.

Miles chose track six: "I Know You by Heart." He and I sang every line with gusto. He knew the lyrics. Every single one.

I promoted him to soul mate when we hit Melissa's driveway.

When he opened my door to help me out of the Camaro and sort of blocked me from passing, I knew something big was about to happen. The girls had obviously detected the thick chemistry we invoked on the dance floor, because they'd advised me to be on high alert for a good-night kiss.

Because the Lord is kind, He distracted me with stellar dancing and beautiful harmonies. It never occurred to me that my friends were being serious. I had never kissed a boy! Before I could even think about what I was supposed to do with my arms or which way I was supposed to tilt my head, I was in a major lip-lock with Miles. Leaning against his car. Which was a Camaro.

I floated into Melissa's house and recited every last detail to my friends, complete with hand gestures and facial expressions for heightened amusement. I went to sleep that night giddy with the reality that I had a boyfriend.

Sadly, no one bothered to tell me that just because a guy kisses you doesn't mean he's bound by the laws of relationship status. This wouldn't have been as big of a deal if I hadn't seen Miles kiss another girl in the school hallway on Monday morning. Right in front of me.

To the bathroom stalls!

I cried for days, listening to my *Beaches* soundtrack on repeat. My sister, Jamie, offered to castrate him, and although her melodramatic heart was in the right place, I chose to process my current adolescent mental state through the written word: I composed a poem.

Every good feeling. Every hurt feeling. It all went into the literary artwork. Many drafts ended up in a fiery chasm (read: Daddy's burn pile), which everyone knows is the only way to destroy painful memories. In the end I had a piece that properly emoted what my tender heart had experienced. I cryptically titled it "The Time."

Did I work through the rhymes and cadence in my diary? Yes.

Did I type the lines out on my electric typewriter? Yes.

Did I recite said poem in class for our prose homework? Yes.

Was Miles in that same class? Sadly, yes.

Just thinking about it gives me the sweats. My throat is thick right now, and I want to lie down, but I must finish this chapter. What kind of person chronicles her first love in the form of a poem and then reads it in front of the guy and a roomful of confused classmates?

A person who feels deeply, that's who.

Would I do it today if I had a modern-day Miles? Probably so. When I say deep, I mean deep.

3

Shake Your Groove Thing

For those of us who LOVE a flash mob

When Sarah Jessica Parker stood in front of her English class and told the other Catholic schoolgirls "I love to dance" in the classic '80s movie *Girls Just Want to Have Fun*, I completely understood the passion behind her simple statement. My soul thrives on eight counts. Give me a stage, some choreography, and a pair of fire-engine-red fringe pants, and I'll whip out a grand jeté on the spot.

I'll injure myself from tip to toe, but that's why we keep ice in the freezer, right? We need it for women in their forties who bust a move without stretching first. And for Mama's famous pink lemonade daiquiris.

Dance is my life. So are those daiquiris.

Sadly, the Lord blocked my dancing machine career path with not one, not two, but three separate knee surgeries. No matter how hard I tried to make it work and ignore the pain, I ended up in some sort of knee brace, crutch, or surgical wing.

The First Injury

The Hallsville Bobcat Belle drill team schedule was a bit of a beast. We practiced at dawn, which meant most of us were sans makeup and still had sponge rollers in our hair so our curls wouldn't be spoiled by the morning dew. While our peers were still in their warm beds, the Belles were high kicking and jump splitting in a field to a recorded cassette tape of the Bobcat band playing our Friday night performance song.

Julie and I stood beside each other in the lineup. We once jump split into a bed of fire ants in that very field. Nothing says *sweet mother of pearl* like a pack of insects invading your personal space.

It was the fall of 1992. Julie and I were sophomores and eagerly anticipating our first homecoming performance as Belles. We were blocking a white-picket-fence routine to the kicky tune of "Wild, Wild West" by Escape Club. Our band played actual songs you could hear on the radio if you listened long enough. It was a nice contemporary supplement to other selections in their repertoire, like the theme from *Star Wars* and "Wipe Out."

The decision to perform a fence routine was carefully calculated. Homecoming calls for the most creative production a team has in their arsenal. It needs to be big and memorable. Winning the halftime show was the goal. White picket fences and the Escape Club were going to get us there.

The week of practice was intense. We planned three girls to each fence, about as high as our waists. We sat on the fences, climbed them, moved them, turned them over, twirled them. And somewhere in the middle, the bravest of the trio on each fence would cartwheel off the top of it, as though she were Mary Lou Retton on the balance beam.

I was chosen to be my trio's brave girl. I distinctly remember our captain, Nicole, asking me to demonstrate how to properly and safely execute the maneuver that was sure to have the crowd explode with a cacophony of praise, while the opposing drill team brooded on the sidelines. Why would they ever choose a hoop routine? What was this, 1983? Amateurs.

I cartwheeled over and over and over. I helped the girls who were scared. I spotted the ones who needed an extra push. I cheered for the ones who flew through the air with ease.

You should have seen our finale. We knew it was good. All the girls marched our fences into one long row that stretched from one thirty-yard line to the other thirty-yard line. Then all fifty-four of us stepped up on the fences, in perfect unison, and hooked arms.

Because we were the best dancers in all the land, we started to high kick. On a fence. Just like the Rockettes—if the Rockettes were cool enough to dance with shabby-chic props like a white picket fence.

Friday night lights are a real thing in Texas. Even if your football team doesn't have a chance of scoring a touchdown, the entire town comes out to the stadium to watch the boys try, the band march, the cheerleaders tumble, the majorettes twirl, and the drill team dance.

As halftime approached, we marched down from the bleachers single file, grabbed our fences, strutted around the end zone on the track, and stood on the sidelines waiting for the last down to be played. When the whistle blew, we took our fences, spotted our yard line, and focused our minds—smiling the entire time, of course.

Citizens of Hallsville, Texas, and esteemed visitors from out of town, prepare to be blown away!

My sequins sparkled under the stadium lights, accentuating my pristine boots and hat. I was living in the wild, wild west, and I was ready to shake what my mama gave me.

Things were going along swimmingly. My fellow fencers were sharp, enthusiastic, and hitting every mark. We could tell the crowd was loving it, and I couldn't wait to hear the response from the big cartwheel.

Here I goooooo! Perfect dismount!

I immediately ignored the loud gunshot sound, assuming someone was hunting nearby. It was East Texas, after all. My brain didn't consider that irregular noise a priority as we were marching our fences up for the long line finish.

I climbed our fence and hooked up with my trio. What talent! I stood on my left leg and kicked my right leg. It was gorgeous! I stood on my right leg and kicked my left leg. *Wait a minute . . .*

And that's when my side of the very long line fell off our fences like dominoes. One by one. Belle down, Belle down, Belle down.

I single-handedly ruined the homecoming halftime show. Once my brain caught up with my body, I realized I couldn't walk. I made eye contact with my captain and told her with my stare—and green face—that I wasn't going anywhere.

A handful of guys helped the Bobcat Belles with a variety of tasks, such as hauling white picket fences into the stadium and setting them up by the scoreboard. In no part of that nonexistent job description did it say you would have to trot out onto the field and carry an injured dancer back to the stands.

Although that would be oh so cool to be swept up into a handsome boy's arms and whisked away. Can you imagine?

I can't either. That's not how it went.

To the young man who was charged with the task, I apologize from the bottom of my heart. I'm sorry trying to hoist me up into your arms proved to be futile since I weighed more than you. I admire your effort and salute your determination.

Question: Did I puke on you? Details are fuzzy, but thanks to Julie's mom, who recorded our entire high school experience, I'm sure we can check the VHS tape. I submitted your name to be included in the Hallsville Bobcat Belles Hall of Fame. You deserve all the accolades.

There I was, watching my knee swell bigger and bigger and bigger as my fellow Belles formed some sort of victory line for the homecoming court. My friend Chance showed up to make sure I was okay and to ask if I was still going to the dance after the game. *Duh, Chance. Is Zack Morris the reason we watch* Saved by the Bell? *Yeah, I'm going.*

My mom never came to the stands because she was watching the wrong thirty-yard line and had no idea it was me who took down an entire row of dancers. I was super chill when she finally got word that her kid was the one with a bum knee. I couldn't miss the homecoming dance. I had the perfect outfit.

It was an Esprit black-and-white block tee with black shorts. Julie helped me decide between black socks with white Keds and white socks with black Keds. Thank goodness for choices. We decided on the latter, and a ginormous bow on my head completed the ensemble. There was just one minor problem.

I couldn't walk.

Never fear! Chance and Matt to the rescue! Each boy took a side and carried me across the street to the school. The party was bumpin' thanks to a Bobcat win. I sat in a chair and tried not to cry as everyone else danced around me.

On Monday, my mom took me to the doctor to ask why her daughter's knee was the size of a basketball. One MRI later he confirmed that my ACL (anterior cruciate ligament) had snapped. So *that* was the shotgun sound I heard! Surgery was inevitable, and the doctor had an opening on Wednesday.

So long, drill-team season. Hello, straight-leg brace.

The Second Injury

I went to a Baptist college. Baptists aren't supposed to dance, but I tore my ACL the second time while dancing at my Baptist college.

Why, Lord? Why?

Madame Dubois counted us off, and one by one, we took turns leaping across the room in ballet class. Step, leap, step, leap, step, crunch. I knew immediately that my indestructible ACL from 1992 had just crapped out on me six years later. I sat down and cried for many reasons, but here are four of them:

1. The pain was excruciating.
2. The All-University Sing competition was only months away, and my sorority had a stellar routine that year. Who could resist dancing and singing street urchins? No one. Who was the co-chairman of the group in charge of choreography? This girl. Who would have to perform in the background on crutches for thirty seconds of the eight-minute piece? Little Orphan Lincee.
3. Straight-leg braces are torture devices, but the bendy machines in hospitals are the devil's playground. The idea of spending months and months in either one produced a fresh flow of salty tears.
4. Physical therapy is where dreams go to get knocked down (but hopefully get up again).

The day I hobbled into the PT center after my roommate Caroline dropped me off, I was mentally prepared for my hour of misery. I hopped up onto the table, flung my huge knee around, and braced myself for someone to push me to the brink of throat punching. Angie was my therapist, and I thought she took a little too much pleasure sticking little pads to my atrophied muscles before cranking up a tiny battery pack that shocked my quads into attention.

A few days into my rehab, Angie didn't show up with her stupid little machine. I asked the kid intern if Angie had skipped town. This kid knew things. Ignoring the fact that we were the same age but I still called him "kid," he leaned in to break the news. Angie no longer worked there.

Then sings my soul!

My heart could barely handle the good news. I was in the best mood, and I couldn't foresee the session getting any better. But then because the Lord is good to me and He wanted me to know that I didn't trash my knee for a second time because I was dancing at a Baptist school, He introduced William into my life.

How do I describe William? Well, he was probably in his midtwenties, and he was attractive. Think Ryan Gosling's face with Chris Pine's eyes on the body of a strong swimmer and the confidence of a hot fireman. He had Chris Pratt's humor, Jim Halpert sarcasm, and Matthew McConaughey's accent. William drove a truck and helped people for a living. Although playing a round of Trivial Pursuit never came up in our hour-long therapy sessions, I'm sure he would have dominated. Only brilliant people work in the medical field.

In short, if I drove to the store, purchased all the ingredients for Lincee's perfect man, mixed them up in a bowl, and baked them in a Pyrex dish at 350 degrees, I would pull William from the oven forty-five minutes later.

Dressing for physical therapy became a fashion priority. Nike shorts and Pi Beta Phi tanks would no longer do. I slowly introduced trendy cut-off denim shorts and cute tops. I opted for a curly ponytail and took five minutes to slap on some makeup. I also relentlessly shaved my legs. Angie often worked with stubbly forests of leg hair during her sessions. Not William. Tuesdays and Thursdays called for the non-disposable razor to always be on hand.

I adored William. He made the physical therapy center my new happy place. Woefully, we arrived at a point in my rehab when I was forced to sign the dismissal forms that stated I had officially been released from William's care. I owed it to William to show him that he was my hero and that my knee was stronger than ever thanks to his careful squat regimen.

I borrowed my friend Kimberly's karaoke machine and recorded myself singing "Wedding Bell Blues" by the 5th Dimension. Why did I choose such a random song from 1969 with which to embarrass myself?

I blame Vada. Vada Sultenfuss.

Yeah, yeah, who's Vada Sultenfuss? She's the tween from the 1991 punch-to-the-gut cryfest *My Girl* starring Anna Chlumsky and Macaulay Culkin—before he dropped off everyone's radar.

Vada has fallen hard for her teacher, and the only way she knows how to trudge through the overabundance of feelings in her adolescent heart is to put on a record and sing "Wedding Bell Blues" at the top of her lungs.

Hey, if it's good enough for Hollywood, it's good enough for me. I sang over the vocals of the 5th Dimension as the karaoke machine recorded my bold profession of love.

Unfortunately, legal mumbo jumbo precludes me from including the lyrics to this mighty gem of a song in this chapter. Since we've come this far down Lord, Help Her Lane, though, I would encourage you to look up the first few stanzas and the chorus so you can fully appreciate what Vada and I were feeling.

I'll help you assess the damage.

I profess my endless love for William. (Good, good.) I'm pretty sure "passion eyes of May" is a poem, so that makes me a literary genius. There's a slight pushiness and frustration surrounding me never seeing William on our wedding day. (Easy, Lincee.) I'm on William's side! (Hooray!) I remind him that he was a loser at some point (ouch!), and I promise to never scheme or lie, which is considerate. Then I end by snubbing his make-out game (not ideal) before offering him an ultimatum.

What boy wouldn't appreciate this musical message?

I carefully place a dozen heart stickers on the cassette tape and hitch a ride to therapy. William is extra beautiful today. I take that as a sign from the Lord that the ultimatum will end in my favor. I stretch out our last moments together, high five him for three months of solid work, and quickly hand him the cassette tape and Pi Phi T-shirt that read "It's just a crush, not a commitment" on the back.

That was the last I ever saw of William. Shocker, I know. I heard he started dating one of the Baylor softball girls who jacked up her rotator cuff.

Her personal musical recording must have been great.

The Third Injury

A group of us went to Cuba on a mission trip in 2010. I've been on a handful of mission trips in my day, and each one has been drastically different. The students I encountered that week weren't like any I've ever met. More than three hundred of them attended an incognito Bible camp, and they lived and breathed the Word that entire week. The joy of worshiping with others unlike me was life-changing. I'll never forget it.

In a region of the world that appeared to be stuck in the 1950s, I soaked up every bit of culture the country had to offer. We were there to support and encourage those attending the camp, but that didn't stop me from absorbing the beautiful beaches, amazing food, incredible architecture, and intoxicating music.

On our last day on the island, our group settled in the lobby of our run-down hotel. The week had been successful, but especially challenging. We'd fought food poisoning and broken-down vehicles, and we'd had a few hospital stays. The trip wasn't a vacation, of course, but we wanted to spend our last night experiencing the city.

Also, a few people had purchased rum and cigars, forgetting they couldn't take those items out of Cuba. Whoopsie. What's a group of friends to do?

Bartender! Eight glasses and a book of matches, please!

You haven't lived until you've smoked a Montecristo and sipped a Cuba Libre next to a 1957 royal-blue Chevy Bel Air.

Back in the hotel lobby, as the evening stretched into night, I noticed some old Cuban women pushing tables to the edge of the walls, making room for a trio of even older men. One carried a trumpet, another some bongos, and a third sat down at the piano. The trio began to play, and life filled that room. Our fellow lobby patrons nimbly made their way to the improvised dance floor and began to mambo with multiple partners.

It looked like so much fun, so I claimed a spot on the floor when a darling Cuban boy asked me in broken English to dance. How else was I supposed to respond? I put down my adult beverage and handed my cigar to the good buddy sitting next to me. Obviously.

I believe we were salsa dancing, but my mind isn't sharp on the details. I was trying hard to remember the specifics of the horrific sequel to *Dirty Dancing*. This was my own personal *Havana Nights*, and I wanted to make the most of it.

My friend Todd grabbed my hand to join the fun. Todd is one of those guys who suffers from Gloria Estefan-itis. The rhythm gets him every time. Luckily for us, he also knows the basic steps to any dance genre. We ball-changed to our hearts' delight and spun around the floor like locals.

My knee gave out during one boisterous twirl. There was some pain. I ignored it. *Havana Nights*, people!

When I walked into my hotel room later, my friend Catha looked at my leg with a little too much disgust for my taste. She cried, "What did you do to your knee?" I looked down and watched as it continued to swell.

I found a pleasant doctor with a gentle bedside manner in the States—pleasant meaning, "Your MRI shows a disgusting mess inside" and gentle like, "You have the knee of a sixty-year-old woman."

I won't bore you with all the medical details. All you need to know is that Todd technically did not cause my ligament to pop by flinging me across the floor. And I was an ACL savant, so I knew what it felt like. My doctor did say my ACL was flopping around like a loose rubber band. Ergo, my kneecap was flopping around too.

Normal people who undergo ACL surgeries are typically told their knee will be stronger than ever. I'm here to tell you that I'm not a normal person. Not only do my supposedly stronger ligaments tear willy-nilly, but the last time I was on Vicodin, I saw Care Bears in my bedroom.

There's Tenderheart and Funshine. Oh look! Cheer Bear has come to check on me too. How thoughtful.

I also swear on my favorite pair of J.Crew jeans that inside the knock-off Thomas Kinkade painting I procured from Hobby Lobby with a 50-percent-off coupon, the campfire was actually burning. I saw the smoke.

It's true. I'm a freak of nature. Apart from the Care Bear sightings and useless ligaments, dissolvable stitches don't dissolve in me.

This makes post-surgery appointments super fun.

Lincee: "What am I supposed to do about the stitches?"
Nurse: "Oh sweetie, you have no stitches to worry about. They're in the inside of your incision. They'll dissolve."

Lincee: "But what if they don't?"
Nurse: "Ha, ha, ha, ha . . . Silly girl."

Lincee: "No, seriously. They didn't dissolve last time."
Nurse: "What? Did you tell the doctor?"

Lincee: "Yes, Nurse Skeptical, I did. He told me it had been ten years since my last ACL surgery and that I shouldn't worry."
Nurse: "Oh. Okay. Then don't worry. But if you see a stitch, do not pull it! Just snip it with scissors and call us."

Two days later, I spied what appeared to be fishing line sticking out of the end of my incision. Of course. Also, gross.

I boosted my leg up onto the bathroom countertop for a better look. The stitch was now curled. Great. Following the nurse's instructions, I attempted to pull the stitch taut enough to snip it. Two inches of stitch rose from the wound as though I were pulling dental floss.

I slowly lowered my leg and closed my eyes. I thought, *I've got to snip it. Snip the stitch, woman! What are you waiting for?*

Naturally, the scissors weren't in their appropriate place in my bathroom. I walked around my apartment gingerly, trying not to hurl while desperately looking for anything resembling scissors.

Finally, I remembered the pair in the wooden block in the kitchen that holds all the fancy knives I never use. Pressing on with my quest, I felt the wispy fishing line wafting around, tickling my leg.

Must. Find. Scissors.

For the second time in ten minutes, I chucked my leg up onto a counter—this time in the kitchen—and forced myself to just power through this minor medical emergency. I did *not* pull the string. I simply held it and snipped right by the incision, and then I placed my leg back on the floor.

Is it hot in here? Why are the lights slowly dimming? Is the ceiling rising or is the floor sinking?

I sort of slid down the general area of the stove/dishwasher and sat on the linoleum, coaxing my head to rest between my legs. But my right leg couldn't bend that way at the moment. The left leg would have to do.

Clamminess and nausea struck next, so I made the decision to go full-on horizontal. I noticed a dehydrated grape and a lone Honey Nut Cheerio tucked in the corner of the baseboards. I mentally made a note to myself to remedy that once I regained consciousness. I spent the night on the kitchen floor with my favorite Care Bears, using a dish towel that read "If I die at Walmart, drag my body to Nordstrom" as a pillow.

The next morning I called the doctor's office.

Lincee: "I need to speak with my doctor, please."
Nurse: "Can I help you with something?"

Lincee: "Nope. I just need to talk to him."
Nurse: "May I tell him what this is regarding?"

Lincee: "I had knee surgery. I have questions about my stitches."
Nurse: "What's wrong with your stitches, honey?"

Lincee: "They're coming out."
Nurse: "Oh girl! Hold on."

The nurse forgets to put me on hold. Therefore, I hear this entire conversation:

Nurse: "Hey. There's a girl who says her stitches are coming out!"
Other Voice: "Was it a knee surgery?"

Nurse: "Yes."
Other Voice: "Then her stitches are not on the outside. Tell her that. They're on the inside. She doesn't come in to have them taken out because they'll dissolve."

Then they laugh at me. They laugh at the freakazoid who will inevitably be featured in at least two medical journals.

Nurse: "Miss Ray? Your stitches are on the inside. They'll dissolve."

Lincee: "Clearly not since I pulled out a long string the length of my arm last night and more is poking out this morning. Now, I'm telling you that dissolvable stitches do not dissolve in my body. I need to know if I'm snipping stitches that are no longer holding anything together and if my insides will soon ooze out of my wound. Does your colleague know how to handle that situation?"

Nurse: "Can you come in today?"

Lincee: "I would be delighted."

Three different types of dance. Three knee surgeries. What did I gain from these experiences? Incredible memories, fun stories, an unceasing love for dance, and the ability to predict the weather.

4

Black Map Dot

For those of us who **LOVE** *small-town life*

Living in a small town has its perks. Throw a rock, and you have a decent chance of hitting a cousin, an aunt, or an uncle. There's always somewhere to go, somewhere to hide, and someone to feed you. Giving directions is easy because all routes stem from the red light downtown or the railroad tracks.

Life slows down when you escape the big city. Neighbors have face-to-face conversations, and an ingrained hospitality surfaces naturally. Everyone embraces the town traditions and volunteers to help. And even though it sounds completely fabricated, it's comforting to know you can go to a place where everybody knows your name.

Other than the fact that I was related to half of the population and I had to scrutinize our extensive family tree before I decided to put forth any effort liking a boy from a distance, I loved growing up in Hallsville.

The beautification committee recently upgraded our holiday decorations that hang from the electric poles up and down Main

Street. They used to be candy canes. Now they're golden trees. This change bothers old curmudgeons in the town like Johnny Ray, who shook his head upon seeing a gold tree instead of a green tree and muttered, "I don't know what message they're trying to send."

My guess is "Merry Christmas," but you brood away, Daddy. And don't be surprised if three ghosts come visit you tonight.

We have a Sonic and a Dairy Queen. You can find any church denomination you want, and Tommy can change your oil down at the Chevron station.

Western Days weekend is a phenomenon you should schedule on your calendar right now. We have a Civil War reenactment complete with working cannons, football, two-stepping to the beat of a live band at the street dance, a cow plop drop, and the Miss Hallsville pageant.

I entered the pageant my senior year. I was runner-up. I'm pretty sure I didn't win because I rated world peace somewhere below a date with Brandon Walsh and a lifetime supply of Krispy Kreme donuts.

We have no shortage of jobs in Hallsville. Why, you can haul hay or bag groceries at the market. You can teach gymnastics or babysit. As in my case, you can be an auto bank teller and freak out the entire population by accidentally activating a silent alarm that indicates the bank is being robbed.

You will also never live that down.

I would like to emphasize once again to those who worked with me at Hallsville's First State Bank that I continue to firmly stand by my defense of the "incidents" that occurred on or around June 1996. No one in our training sessions told me we had an emergency call button under the teller counter. Will you continue to chastise me for crossing my legs that legendary day, accidentally pressing the button one may utilize if masked bandits hold up the place? I think not. How was I supposed to know our small town implemented such elaborate technology?

Also, no one told me that closing the blinds in the front office is a super-secret signal to the outside world that we're being robbed on the inside. The afternoon sun was in my eyes. The action of simply adjusting the blinds seemed harmless at the time. If anything, we should applaud the prompt police officer who showed up instantly to check out the situation.

Silver lining, people.

It's a Moo Point

You can probably talk your way out of a speeding ticket if you play your cards right, which can help you make it to a pasture party on time. An entire town's worth of people can also help you in any emergency situation.

I know this because Johnny Ray is a walking emergency situation.

Daddy returned to the house one day and busted through the front door in a panic. "There's a dead cow, and her baby is trying to nurse. I need help separating them. Get in the Jeep."

No words have ever terrified me more. I stood completely still, hoping he would give up on me and move on to someone else who had an iron stomach. He didn't, though, because I was the only person in the house. He kept yelling at me, holding up his broken finger.

I use the term "broken" because there's not a word for when you cut off your own finger and then a doctor sews it back on. No joke. Daddy caught his finger in a hay baler, and then he sawed it off with a pocket knife, picked it up off the ground, drove to the house, and made my sister take him to the emergency room so some "Doogie Howser–looking doctor" could reattach it to his hand.

I began stuttering, telling my dad I wasn't the best person for this job, and that he would be better off just letting the dead cow decompose on its own. Also, what about the little baby, and could we feed it with a bottle?

Daddy: "You have exactly two minutes to find someone to help me, or you have a choice to either wrangle a calf or haul a dead cow."

I flew to the phone and called every boy in my high school graduating class, but not one answered. Not one. *Where have all the good men gone, for crying out loud? Literally one to four of them are swimming in my pool or fishing in the pond every time I turn around.*

I silently cursed my boyfriend for having the audacity to go on a camping trip that weekend. Then it dawned on me. My boyfriend had brothers. Brothers who were younger, unwise, and probably bored. *Call them!*

Within minutes, Jeremy and an entourage of friends were out at the farm, circled around the deceased, and assessing the situation. Daddy was manhandling the baby with one arm as I held the two-month-old blue heeler puppy who kept trying to nip at the calf's hooves.

Jeremy grabbed a thick chain from the back of my dad's Jeep, and then wrapped it around the cow's neck and dragged it away on his friend's four-wheeler. It was a good day for these young high school kids. My dad became a legend in hushed circles. I'm glad they have stories to share around the campfire.

What Will Your Verse Be?

I like that most people know who I am and that we never have to lock the doors. It's a simpler life. Listen for the train in the distance. Catch fireflies and put them in a Mason jar. Explore the woods and eat wild blackberries.

Not many kids can say they went to the school in the same town from kindergarten through twelfth grade. The education I received from dedicated teachers inside the walls of Hallsville classrooms helped mold me into the woman I am today. Countless individuals from the school district poured into me, challenged me, pushed me, and celebrated my achievements.

None more than my eccentric senior year English teacher, Mrs. Lee.

I had never seen the movie *Dead Poets Society* until she showed it to us in class. When Robin Williams's character, Professor Keating, tells his classroom full of people-pleasing students, "No matter what anybody tells you, words and ideas can change the world," I sat a little straighter. I leaned a little closer. I listened a little harder.

Mrs. Lee was a hundred years old, looked like Cinderella's fairy godmother, and taught exactly one honors English class at Hallsville High School. She also completely believed with all her heart that she could correctly predict the future. She told me I would marry a man wearing a white lab coat who lived in a big home with tiny fossils and footprints pressed into the concrete of the living room floor.

If you're a doctor with an enthusiasm for the study of archaeology, over the age of forty, and reading this blessed book about love, I'd like to introduce myself. I'm Lincee, and I'm not dangerous or a psycho. Let's meet for frozen yogurt, because I'm the only human in the world who doesn't frequent Starbucks on a regular basis for a nice cup of burnt water.

We all loved Mrs. Lee. She encouraged those of us with a creative streak to approach our studies in unconventional ways. For example, she gave us a choice when it came to tests. We could either take a written exam or turn in a video depicting all the lessons learned from the piece of literature.

Two brilliant classmates, Gene and Adrian, approached Julie and me about teaming up to submit our final on *Pygmalion* as a video. I can still remember Julie yelling at the horses in the pasture next to my house, "Come on, Dover! Move your bloomin' arse!"

We may have thrown some *My Fair Lady* references in there for comic relief, but Mrs. Lee enjoyed every second of our masterpiece.

Our wonderful teacher encouraged us to look at our lives through a different lens. She knew we had potential and that a great big world was out there just waiting for us to make our mark. She gave us permission to be ourselves and freedom to branch out a bit beyond our comfort zones. I had no idea at the time, but her entire class was a lesson on carpe diem. For a bunch of kids from a one-red-light town, this was an extremely important part of our education.

Pointing to a class photo of alumni from long ago, Professor Keating says to his students,

> Look at them. . . . The world is their oyster. They believe they're destined for great things, just like many of you. Their eyes are full of hope, just like you. Did they wait until it was too late to make from their lives even one iota of what they were capable? Because, you see, gentlemen, these boys are now fertilizing daffodils. But if you listen real close, you can hear them whisper their legacy to you. Go on, lean in. Listen. You hear it? . . . Carpe diem. Seize the day, boys. Make your lives extraordinary.

Mrs. Lee helped us consider the possibility of making our lives extraordinary, and it worked. I think back to all my friends in that class and smile at the phenomenal things they're doing with their lives. I'm so glad Gene was compassionate enough to arrange for a proper send-off on our last day in Mrs. Lee's class. One by one, we all stood on our desks and exalted her with a heartfelt "O Captain! My Captain!" I still get a little teary thinking about it.

A squishy grandma English teacher in a town with a little more than a thousand people at the time helped me embrace my love of words.

I find great comfort in Professor Keating's charge to his students:

> We don't read and write poetry because it's cute. We read and write poetry because we are members of the human race. And the

human race is filled with passion. And medicine, law, business, engineering, these are noble pursuits and necessary to sustain life. But poetry, beauty, romance, love—these are what we stay alive for. . . . You are here. Life exists. . . . The powerful play goes on, and you may contribute a verse. . . . What will your verse be?

Hallsville gave me roots. It also gave me wings.

5

Shalom, Y'all

For those of us who LOVE a place we don't call home

We all have that place we love that's not home, yet our heart feels at ease when we're there. It might be your grandparents' rickety old lake house or a log cabin in the snowy Colorado mountains. Or a place where the surf forces sand between your toes as you breathe in the salty sea air.

Life makes sense in that corner of the world. An uncanny peace accompanies you, and your brain makes crazy suggestions like *I could live here*, because the people accept you as their own.

For me, this place is the Holy Land.

If you ever have the opportunity to go there, I suggest you do it, and you're in for a treat if your itinerary includes the majestic city of Petra. It's one of the eight wonders of the world and truly a sight to behold. It's also where *Indiana Jones and the Last Crusade* was filmed.

The first thing I did when I entered the city was imagine I was a college professor, sans fedora and bullwhip. Our tour guide was kind to indulge those of us who pretended to be running from a giant boulder. He also mentioned that I must make the trek up to the Monastery after lunch, because it would change my life forever. Who am I to turn down an opportunity like that? I congregated with others from our group at the base of the mountain and began the journey at an aggressive pace. Very few of us considered that the climb takes forty minutes and boasts more than eight hundred steps that zigzag up high inclines.

Pretty much immediately, the slight throbbing pain in my bum knee told me to take my time. I convinced myself I was just stopping to enjoy the view as the other people my age passed me left and right. The first ten minutes weren't that bad. The second ten minutes? Not so much. I started doing that fake "Oh, look at that rock!" or "Check out this view!" as I leaned over, huffing and puffing, convinced that my right lung was about to explode in my chest.

I asked my fellow climbers, one an eighty-year-old man who was on the waiting list for a kidney, to take my picture at every curve we rounded. These precious seconds allowed me to catch my breath and chug down ridiculous amounts of water. I think around forty-three photos of me were taken on the way up that mountain, which were all immediately deleted.

Reaching the thirty-minute mark, I almost decided to take up residency with the Bedouins who peddled hookah pipes every hundred yards. I was resting against a rock in the blistering heat when a nice lady offered me shade under her tent. I collapsed onto her blankets and went fully horizontal. She offered me tea and even let me bounce her baby for a few minutes before I returned to the mountain that knows no mercy.

Another one hundred yards at the next Bedouin tent, a little boy tried to force a camel-tooth necklace on my arm. After I graciously declined, he said, "That's okay, miss. Only five more minutes left. You come see me when you are done!"

If I could have lifted my arms, I would have picked up that little eight-year-old and carried him on my shoulders to the promised land. This information gave me a new sense of strength. I readjusted my backpack, and then I daintily dabbed the sweat from my brow and trudged on.

The next Bedouin tent resident was an old lady smoking the largest joint in existence. I bet she had a few offers for it, but that's neither here nor there.

Bedouin: "Miss? Miss? Something to take home?"
Lincee: "No, thank you. I'm just going to the top of the Monastery. I hear it's going to change my life."
Bedouin: "Okay. Only five more minutes."

Hold the phone. Five more minutes was five minutes ago.

While I was calculating what it would take for me to fling myself off the cobbled steps into the death valley below, I was rescued by the fairest angel this side of the evil mountain.

His name was Christian. I assume he sensed my internal struggle and clearly recognized my physical inability to press on. He offered, nay, insisted that he carry my backpack the remaining eternal five minutes.

A huge weight was literally lifted off my shoulders, because my laptop, camera, thirty-two-pound Bible, and seventeen Bedouin necklaces were weighing me down more than I can tell you. I skipped along to the end of the path, light on my feet and sipping my water from a bottle with glee, while encouraging Christian to the top. My moving cover of "Hero" by Enrique Iglesias was abruptly cut short, however, by the view that towered before me.

The Monastery was huge. It took my angel Christian and another jock dude to boost me up into this beautiful building to take a closer look. Sadly, it smelled like urine in there, so I opted to soak in the majesty outside from a nearby rock.

The task of walking back down the mountain was easier on the lungs, but much more strenuous on the knee with the previously torn ACL. It was pleading with me to rest, ice, compress, and elevate. Riding a camel never sounded so good, and I was relieved to find a herd waiting for me at the exit.

I rode a black one named ZaZa. Our guide said she was the best camel in Petra and was considered a matriarch of the herd. She was also impatient. ZaZa insisted on being first in line, so she would annoyingly pass other camels to make her way to the front. Since we were tethered together, this made for me some awkward maneuvering among our group. A man's legs became wedged between his camel and mine, the other camels would spit and hiss at ZaZa for not staying in a straight row, and I would often have to swing my legs from one side to the other so I wouldn't knock over Bedouin displays of Petra magnets and oil lamps.

Back at the hotel, after showering and de-camelizing myself, my friend Nancy Jane and I joined our group downstairs for dinner and a debriefing of the day's events. We closed out the evening with cocktails in the Jordanian-inspired hookah pipe room, while Ali and his guitar assistant Mohammed played a rotating repertoire of exactly three songs: "The Girl from Ipanema," "God Bless the USA," and "Every Step You Take."

Conversation was light because we were all nursing bruised tailbones, camel-horn blisters, swollen knees, sunburns, and donkey rot. We were also unable to complete sentences because we were high from the secondary hookah smoke.

All the girls looked fabulous, however, with our camel-tooth necklaces.

Rebel with a Cause

My trip to Israel was filled with boisterous laughter, poignant moments, and a barrage of useless information. *Yes, I do want to see the field where David fought Goliath, but I really don't care about visiting the rock where John the Baptist's cousin may or may not have stopped to tie his sandal.*

Oh, I've got a dozen of those examples.

There's the time our tour guide, Ruti, told us about Israeli archaeologist Claire Epstein. You probably remember her from your ancient history ruins class in college. Didn't we all take that our junior year? She's the lucky lady who found an identical pair of stone lions that guarded the city of Hazel while she was "easing" herself in a bush near the excavation site. Shaloms all around for Claire!

Would you like to hear about the time I ate St. Peter's Fish at a gas station restaurant on a lonely Capernaum highway? They let us decide if we wanted to include the head. How courteous.

Or I could give you step-by-step instructions on how to make Mama Druise's unleavened bread. I picked up this recipe at the local shop where Mama Druise works behind the counter by the cigarettes. It's super easy.

1. Remove shoes. Squat down on the floor near Jewish Coke machine and place round seat cushion from outdoor patio on a bucket in front of you.
2. Mold the dough into a large circle, making sure to cover the circumference of the seat cushion.
3. Remove and unleaven.
4. Smear on a little goat cheese and a cup and a half (or two) of extra virgin olive oil.
5. You may substitute goat cheese with Nutella.
6. Wrap and hand to hungry customer.

So straightforward. So practical.

Would you like to break the law in Tiberias? I've done it. Boy, was that a hoot. After a day of baking in the sun, sweating olive oil, and having typical Holy Land fun, a bunch of us wanted to go swimming in the Sea of Galilee. Sadly, even though our hotel abutted the lake, it had no access to the beach on which we could frolic. A chain-link fence hindered us from our quest.

Normal people take a ten-minute walk to enter the beach legally from a public gate. Nancy Jane and I aren't those people.

We spied a family fishing on the wall of rocks next to the beach and decided to go down to see if we could sweet-talk our way into a shortcut. Much like we questioned the black curly hairs on the ceiling of our hotel room, we wondered, *How did they get there?* A sign read "Trespassers will be forced to hike to the Monastery again" in Hebrew.

Nancy Jane, in her best Southern drawl and pleasant voice, introduces herself to the mother, who happens to be on our side of the fence.

Nancy Jane: "Shalom! How do we get over there?"

The mom looks confused. I take over, using sign language, my best charade moves, and my most effective emphases.

Lincee: "*How* did *they* [point to family] get *over* [make a hand gesture like a rainbow] the *fence* [touch fence]?
Mom: "*Ah-gch!*" (Hebrew for "aha")

She makes the universal sign for climbing a ladder, and we all hop the fence, ignoring the warning sign. Nancy Jane and I find ourselves among the true riffraff of Tiberias: The rule-breaker mom's family, fishing. High school girls in revealing bikinis, sunbathing. A questionable man on a wave runner, trying to get Nancy Jane to "take a ride with him" tonight. She graciously declines.

We careen down the huge wall of jagged rocks to say we've dipped a toe in the Galilee. About halfway down, I hear Nancy Jane talking slowly to someone. I look up to see a young Jewish kid carrying on an enthusiastic conversation in another language.

Afraid that he would push her off the rock wall to her death, I make my way back up to find a larger crowd of six Jewish boys. Only one speaks broken English, but we all tried our best to communicate. I'm pretty sure I agreed to marry the one in a Phillies T-shirt when he comes of age. Oy vey.

The Holy City or Hosanna!

I may have eaten the face of a fish, broken the law by hopping a fence, and nearly died at a major motion picture movie location, but I also walked where the Lord walked. I watched a beautiful sunset over the Mediterranean. I floated in the Dead Sea. I took communion at a tomb where Jesus might have been buried and rose again.

Shepherds' Field in Bethlehem gave me a new perspective on Psalm 23. A boat ride on the Sea of Galilee reminded me that even though Peter stepped on the water and then sank when he took his eyes off Jesus, he had the faith to step out.

I was also baptized in the Jordan River, but I've never written about the experience. What I felt is indescribable.

My journey to Israel took the clinical and made it tangible, the tangible and made it meaningful. When I walked where Jesus walked, I realized my need for Scripture and the love for my Savior had been reignited. I've never learned so much, laughed so hard, and been so convicted in such a short amount of time.

More importantly, the Holy Land opened my eyes to what it means to serve others well. Sitting on a bench in the middle of the Garden of Gethsemane, I prayed for the Lord to open my eyes and prepare my heart for mission work. I asked Him to help me understand Matthew 28:19: "Go and make disciples of all the nations."

I officially had the "go" part down. It was time to tackle that "make disciples" bit.

6

Hands and Feet

For those of us who **LOVE** *to serve*

The first person I remember truly serving with all my heart was my sister, Jamie. She would time her baby sister with her Swatch watch to see how long it took me to run downstairs and make her a sandwich. I did this on numerous occasions.

Another time I remember serving others was when my class sang "Jingle Bells" in Spanish at the old folks' home. My East Texas accent added another layer to a musical event that was already confusing enough for most of the residents.

The next couple of years were sprinkled with different out-reaches, although I wouldn't technically call them service. They were more like prepping for college application essays or real-world resumes. I volunteered with food banks, read to a couple of kids a few times, and even picked up trash in the city park.

I was pleasantly surprised to learn that serving others came easy to me. When I learned during a church Bible study that serving is off the charts, hands down my spiritual gift, I decided it needed to be a bigger priority in my life. I stepped out of my comfort zone and declared it was time for a change. That change came to fruition thanks to a mission trip to Cuba. Remember? The place where I blew out my knee for the third time?

Ah, memories.

The purpose of our mission trip was to provide the staff of the organization with extra hands and arms, hugs, and general encouragement. Only ten staff members served more than three hundred kids. Our extra fifteen bodies were a welcome addition for small group sessions, extracurricular activities, and meal prep.

The night we arrived at camp, I was nominated to address the audience of Spanish-speaking kiddos. With the help of a fabulous translator, sheer willpower, and prayer, I managed to reassure the students they were safe within those walls and free to worship however they pleased.

Trust me when I say that a huge group of young Cuban believers openly loving the Lord and praising His name in a secure location is awe-inspiring.

On the second day of our trip, three of our key people were struck with what can only be described as the mother of all food poisoning incidents. They were in desperate need of medical attention, and we weren't going to send them to a Cuban hospital by themselves. My friend Catha and I went along to offer moral support.

That morning I had thought about what a privilege it was to wake up every day with nothing more to do than serve others. I didn't have a phone to distract me, a website to maintain, an article to create, or a book to write. I had only me. I hoped I would be enough, and that God would use me mightily on the island.

And that He did. But in a curious way.

I held a bucket as my friend puked over and over. It was almost comical as I followed another friend to the bathroom, holding her saline drip. The Lord also gifted me with a merciful heart. This is exactly where He needed me to be, even though I wanted to practice my Spanish on innocent schoolgirls and had even gone as far as learning how to say "Team Edward" or "Team Jacob" in their native tongue.

By the way, it's *Equipo de Eduardo* and *Equipo de Jacob* in case you need this bit of *Twilight*-related information in your own life, should you be serving in a Spanish-speaking country.

How silly of me to think teenagers would even care about the *Twilight* series at a time like this. These kids traveled many hours to get to this camp, some in the back of trucks where they had to stand the entire time. The facility was less than stellar, but you never heard one complaint from any of them. Not one.

The girls were in dormitories that held about nine bunk beds, two girls to one twin bed. The boys slept on mattresses in the sanctuary. Our staff all slept in a room in one long line of bodies.

Did I mention there was only one bathroom for the girls and only one for the boys? That's two toilets for three hundred people.

God is moving mountains in Cuba, and it was a joy to witness it firsthand. We are so blessed to live in a country where we can pray when we want or sing hymns when we want. We can gather to study the Bible in groups. We can read chapters in books about mission trips or even make the decision to stop reading books that sneak Jesus into the table of contents.

We have been commanded to serve one another. Most of us just need a little push to point us in the right direction. You don't have to get on a plane or cross an ocean. Sometimes the need to serve is in your own backyard.

I'm reminded of one of my favorite quotes from author and speaker Jill Briscoe that I heard at a conference years ago: "You go where you're sent, you stay where you're put, you give what you've got until you're done."

If you don't do your part to help make a difference, who will?

It's Not about Me

The year after my trip to Cuba, I was the community service coordinator for the women at my church. I thought it was my duty to choose an organization to submerge myself in, and I chose Star of Hope women's shelter. My friend Jennifer had the great idea to implement a night of pampering these ladies with manicures and pedicures. I soon learned that some people in this world have a weird foot phobia. Since I don't mind feet, I thought my services would be best used on that detail.

Armed with foot spas and enough Calgon to take the entire room away, a few of us settled on the floor, ready to scrub all troubles into oblivion. I will never forget the lady who hovered behind me. She appeared tired and unclean, and she never sat down. I introduced myself and invited her to sit and soak. She looked at me with glassy eyes and said, "You're doing feet?"

I explained that I was in no way a professional, but that I knew how to swipe some paint on a toenail. Then I babbled on about something that had to do with lavender bubbles and said I was praying that I wouldn't electrocute her with the foot spa. She didn't flinch.

Some people don't understand my other spiritual gift—sarcasm.

Still standing, she looked at me again and said, "You're really going to touch my feet?"

A big lump swelled in my throat. I fought back tears, realizing that she was blown away at the thought of someone washing her feet.

"Yes. Yes, I am," I answered in a whisper.

That's when another shift in my heart occurred. Two nail-pierced hands reached down, touched my face, and said, *I've been waiting for you to finally get it!*

Oh, I get it. It's not about me.

I'd like to let you in on a little secret. I'm a work in progress. I'm not the shiny, happy servant. Yes, I wash feet. Yes, I lead a

Bible study. What you don't know is that I struggle to keep a genuine heart while I serve.

Some days I wonder when life is going to start going my way. Part of me likes to tally all my good deeds and present them to the Lord so I can be rewarded. Haven't I put in enough time at the church? When am I going to be blessed with a husband? What does she do that I don't? How come she gets rewarded and I don't? These ladies' feet aren't going to wash themselves. Does God even see what I'm going through to advance His kingdom?

Does that sound like a heart that serves well?

Then I stop. And confess. I confess my bitter, hard heart daily and ask Him to reveal what it means to be a true servant of God. Then I read Romans 12:1–2 again and again and again:

> Therefore, I urge you, brothers and sisters, in view of God's mercy, to offer your bodies as a living sacrifice, holy and pleasing to God—this is your true and proper worship. Do not conform to the pattern of this world, but be transformed by the renewing of your mind. Then you will be able to test and approve what God's will is—his good, pleasing and perfect will.

It's not about me.

It's about how we are all called to serve others.

It's about surrendering our ways to His ways.

It's about doing something sacrificial.

It's about loving others well.

It's about others seeing Jesus in me.

7

Arise

For those of us who LOVE *the underdog*

I'm surprised Mrs. Lee didn't give me a heads-up about going to Africa with my friend Alissa when she took off her glasses and stared into my soul.

Oh wait. Her prediction about the man in the lab coat didn't come true—at least not yet. Never mind.

I hesitated to join Alissa at first. I had a lot going on at the time, and several projects required my attention. Exactly zero planning had been accomplished for my pending move. Plus, my first book was far from being finished, and no matter how many times I tried to bribe my sister, she refused to be my ghostwriter.

Educating myself on the ins and outs of the Arise Africa ministry we'd be visiting soon dissolved all my anxiety. A strong desire to help replaced my frustration. I realized very little goes a long way over there, and I began to hope. I began to trust. And that gift of mercy came bubbling up again.

One of my favorite wedding reception songs is "I Gotta Feeling." The Black Eyed Peas totally hit pay dirt with that one. It has withstood the test of time. I've shouted the words of this quintessential anthem on various occasions and have specific hand gestures and syncopated shoulder shrugs to certain lyrics. *L'chaim!*

The Peas capitalized on that inner "something" we all hone in on at times. We're excited for the night to come because we know without a doubt it's going to be a good night. It's going to be a good, *good* night. Woo-hoo!

I've experienced these same butterflies when I've spoken publicly. Or when I'm about to hit "publish" on a blog post. Or when Cadbury Creme Eggs hit the grocery store shelves.

Alissa had this feeling after visiting Zambia. It's her "other place" that feels like home. She was frustrated and saddened when she saw children living in extreme poverty. So she listened to that feeling, did a ton of research, prayed through the process, and decided to do something about the injustice.

Some of us start nonprofits in our late twenties; others start blogs. To each her own.

Alissa is the executive director of Arise Africa. In short, it's a ministry based in Zambia that works with orphaned and vulnerable children. Alissa helps them have the life God desires for them.

Alissa was twenty-eight years old when she launched Arise Africa. She juggled her "real" job and the nonprofit, until the Lord blew the organization up, exceeding everyone's expectations. Alissa soon got another nudge and walked away from her career as a photographer for the NBA to cultivate the seeds she'd planted only a year before. She was offering me a chance to see with my own eyes the tangible blessings she'd experienced.

And then the butterflies showed up in full force, a little bit more aggressively than when I watch Sam Heughan in *Outlander*.

The fun fluttering turned into more of a questionable churning sensation that signaled things were about to go down. Or come up.

You bet I gotta feeling. It's called conviction. And it gave me hives.

Since the world had been revolving around me for a long time, though, I decided to take a break from focusing on my life and see others. Africa sounded like the perfect place to do just that. *Pass the malaria pills, people. We're going to Zambia!*

I visited this amazing continent for the first time in 2012. It was a life-changing trip. Each day I wrestled with dozens of emotions. One moment I was overwhelmed by the fact that I'd never really known the true definition of *poverty* until now. The next moment I stood in awe, soaking up the pure joy on faces that was the direct result of sugary lollipops. I was sad when I saw someone in need, and I was inspired when I witnessed others step up to help.

As I sat with sixteen other people in the courtyard of the Arise Africa complex, I asked the others why they signed on for this trip. Some were eager to meet sponsored children face-to-face. Others were curious about the organization and were happy to be along for the ride. Everyone looked forward to spending time with the Arise Africa staff. We were there to help, whatever that looked like. We knew we'd been called to serve, and that's what we were going to do.

For one week, our goal was to take "I" and "me" statements out of the equation. We were simply there to give our time, our strength, our wisdom, and ultimately our hearts to others.

Based on previous experience, I knew some moments wouldn't be easy. I needed to make a conscious decision to lean in and not allow the feeling of uncertainty to win. I needed to concentrate on the good parts. The good, *good* parts. Woo-hoo!

It's also important to remember that actions speak louder than words.

When my older sister and I were little, we loved jumping up and down on her bed. My mom bought it from Sears. Or maybe the Spiegel catalog. Both options seem conceivable. It was beige plastic with a whimsical gossamer canopy. If I jumped high enough, I could touch the white billowy fabric and feel the euphoric sensation of fake flying.

My parents didn't care *if* we jumped on my sister's bed, but they did care *when* we jumped on the bed. One time we enjoyed this random extracurricular activity just as my father was turning in for the night. My sister's bedroom was directly above my parents' bedroom, and the squeaking and creaking became too much for Daddy. When we heard him walking up the stairs, we both plopped down and pulled the covers up under our chins.

He said nothing. He just looked at both of us and raised an eyebrow. We knew what that meant.

Moments after the eyebrow had made an appearance, my sister dared me to take a few more bounces. There was no way Daddy would come upstairs again. I accepted the challenge because Jamie was older and wiser and would never provoke me to make a bad decision.

For the second time in a decade, Daddy came up the stairs and said nothing. He just hung his belt on one beautiful canopy bedpost. It was clear that heads would roll if we even thought about jumping on that bed again.

Sometimes words aren't needed.

I experienced this phenomenon again at a school in Dotroda. When our convoy rolled up through the gate, what felt like hundreds of children in adorable orange-and-brown uniforms swarmed all the white people. Surely this must be what Justin Timberlake feels like every single day.

It's natural for your brain to send panic signals to your body in moments like these. Then you remember that these children may live in an impoverished community, but they've found sanctuary in the form of a mighty school that provides education, food, and spiritual nourishment. Everything outside the school feels daunting. Everything inside the school feels hopeful.

The Dotroda school is light in the middle of a dark place. The students are adorable. The staff are rock stars. A beautiful woman named Brenda gives every bit of her heart and soul to each child. She knows the hairs on their heads. She knows each boy and girl by name, as well as their siblings' names. The passion flows from this woman's body.

The joy you feel in Dotroda is infectious. So much is communicated with just a look or touch, a universal language you fall into when you're serving.

I looked directly into the eyes of those kids and saw endless possibilities. I joined in their laughter. I received enough hugs to fill my bucket for the rest of the year. I held precious hands. I prayed silently over each head. I thanked the Lord for moving mountains and praised His name for transforming all the lives I saw before me.

It's not every day you meet a group of people who all live and breathe the words of John: "Let us not love with words or speech but with actions and in truth" (1 John 3:18).

Sometimes words aren't needed, but other times they stab you straight to the marrow.

Here's a sentence that can make your heart stop for a beat: "He says their parents ran away from them."

I angled myself toward Mama Dailes, who mothers fourteen orphans at the Arise Africa home, and asked her to repeat what she had just translated.

"Their parents just left them. He thinks they ran away."

Two brothers were abandoned on the side of the road in a neighborhood they didn't recognize as their own. Many people said they had been there for weeks. A stranger took them to social welfare, and they were put on TV to see if their parents would see them and come back for them. They didn't. The boys

72

were sent to a transitional home, where it was inevitable that they would be separated.

When Arise Africa heard the news, the general rally cry was, "Not on our watch!"

The staff at Arise Africa picked them up from the transitional home to ensure these brothers would stay together—as a family. No one hesitated. They just responded. What a beautiful example of grace.

When I heard the story, I felt frustrated. My heart ached. Tears welled in my eyes. I wanted to drop to my knees. I wanted to grab both boys and never let go. I wanted to scream "Are you *kidding* me?" to Mama Dailes. I wanted to be able to comfort the boys, but they didn't speak English, and I didn't speak Nyanja.

I wanted to find their parents and shake them, then ask, "How can you choose to walk away from these faces? I've wanted kids my entire life and you just desert the two you have? These perfect, precious boys? You have to be *out of your mind!*"

Instead of saying or doing any of that, I just stared at Lovemore and Munyunda as Mama Dailes shared more of their story.

"They think they see a ghost at night."

Come again, Mama D?

Apparently, the power source of the solar panel in the home had two glowing green lights they could see from their beds. *Of course* this looked like a ghost when these two kids were huddled together in the dark. They'd never lived in a house with electricity, or even running water. Who knew if their home had walls or even a roof? Glowing green lights are what nightmares are made of. Who ya gonna call?

I told Mama D to tell them I was a Ghostbuster and that I had removed all paranormal spirits from the grounds.

Sidebar: Africans I've met don't typically "get" my jokes and sarcasm. Each time I've visited, I've been a hot mess because my approval addiction suffered big-time.

Mama D said, "I told them Jesus lives in this house and He will protect them."

That works too.

Mama D told me for the first couple of nights she'd put the boys' mattresses on the floor in her room. Then the brothers had migrated back to the boys' side of the house to sleep with Fred, who had lived in the house for several years. All three shared a twin bed.

God bless Fred.

At this point, I was an emotional mess. I smiled, patted the boys on the shoulder, and went to the bathroom to cry for a few minutes. Then I washed my face, took a deep breath, and asked myself, *What would Mama Dailes do? What would Fred do?* Then it hit me.

Don't hesitate. Rise up. Serve. Make a difference. Right where I stand, just as I am.

8

Zambian Uber

For those of us who would LOVE
to walk a mile in your shoes

The question was simple: Who would like to shadow an Arise Africa child sponsorship officer and be a CSO for a day?

Yes, please.

My friend Lara and I were paired with Susan, one of the CSOs at the Dotroda school. Alissa told us we needed to get up before the sun to be at the bus stop by 7:00 a.m. We set the alarm for half-past twilight and hopped right out of bed when Lara's phone chimed.

No, we didn't. We ignored the chime.

Instead, we quizzically looked at the country director, Megan, when she barged through the door of our room, wondering why we weren't ready to go. I have never dressed so fast in my entire life. In a matter of minutes, I managed to brush my teeth, put on deodorant, cover my funky hair with a hat, and fill two bottles with water. *Dotroda, here we come!*

Fun fact: I often called this school Dorota. Then I would pause, knowing it wasn't named after Blair Waldorf's maid on *Gossip Girl*. After a few moments, I would work it out. Dorota quickly morphed into Dotroda, and all was well.

We leave the complex at 6:45 a.m. By 7:30 a.m. we meet up with Susan and hop into a minibus (read: it's a van) with seventeen of our closest friends. Lara leans in to whisper, "I wish I had even half a cup of coffee." *I hear you, sister. Except replace the word coffee with Dr Pepper and add a blueberry Pop-Tart to the menu.*

It's important to know that each minibus has a conductor who basically sticks his entire torso out of the moving vehicle's window, hoping to entice another passenger to join the party by whistling at crowds on street corners. When our conductor pounds on the roof of the van, signaling the driver to stop, we're totally surprised by his decision to add yet another adult human being to our masses.

Really, dude? This nice Zambian man to my right's butt cheek is halfway on my lap. And I'm halfway on Lara's. Have you thought through this decision?

Lara happens to be sitting on the makeshift wooden chair that is in no way part of the original schematics of this Honda Odyssey. The conductor instructs the new woman to sit in the row in front of us and then climbs in himself. He doesn't have a chair. He shuts the door before bending over Lara's lap.

I'll let your imagination go where it wants to go after reading that sentence.

Jesus, take the wheel. Really. Take it.

One wrong turn, one illegal jump of a road's median, and thirty minutes later our conductor launches out of the moving van as if he's trying out for the Zambian X-Games. Although Lara is thankful to have her lap back, we are concerned for his well-being. Did he make the jump? Did he drop and roll at the end? Would he medal if given the proper training? We'll never know.

We reach downtown one hour into our journey. It's time to get off this minibus and switch to one going in a different direction. We track Susan's serpentine style. She's the mother hen, and we're her little chicks following behind as she whisks past people selling smartphones, candy, and hair extensions. Luckily, I don't need a cell phone or any new polyester hair. My weave is holding up nicely in the Zambian heat. And everyone who knows me knows I don't travel without candy. I pat my emergency Starburst stash in my satchel and keep moving.

Susan chooses a bus in the back of the pack, wiggles her way into the last row of seats, and settles in for another forty-five minutes of intimacy with complete strangers, swaying to the smooth sounds of Zambia's version of light contemporary hits. Delilah would be so proud.

At 9:15 we arrive at the right neighborhood and schlep our stuff to the Dotroda school. The kids are gearing up for testing, and we find Chris, Joseph, and David in the shipping container that's repurposed as an office, leading them in a devotional. At this point, I'm nursing a caffeine headache and Lara's suffering from thigh violation. We need Jesus, and we need Him bad.

Chris quotes nine thousand verses in five minutes and Joseph brings the Word. David schools us, and Susan inspires everyone in two sentences. It's evident that these blessed individuals know what they're doing. I'm so glad they're in charge of these sweet children who are running around outside like banshees.

The next item on the agenda is chopping vegetables. You've never known the agony of defeat until for a solid forty minutes you've used a dull knife to slice and dice what looks like collard greens, but for some reason is called broccoli. You'll also never feel like more of a weakling than when you see a Zambian woman who could be your mother chop four greens to your one with the same knife. Hallelujah.

At 10:00, we leave the school with Joseph to pick up a kid named Isaiah and his grandmother, so we can take him to a good hospital we trust. He has an open wound on his leg. Joseph introduces me to him as a "Ghostbuster," and I beam. My sarcastic wit is spreading!

Joseph arranges for a taxi to pick us all up from Isaiah's house. We pile into the car, and I hand out pink and red Starburst candy and call it brunch.

We arrive at the hospital forty-five minutes later, only to find that the gaping hole in Isaiah's leg can't be treated. The doctor we typically see isn't in today. We talk the nurses into at least dressing his wound before we hike over to the clinic. While Isaiah waits his turn, he has the distinct displeasure of witnessing another kid having blood drawn. Consider his mind blown. This should be fun.

We get back into a cab and head to the clinic. On the way, we pass a lake, and Lara asks its name.

Joseph: "That's sewage."

Good. To. Know. Put away the bathing suits, ladies.

An hour later, we arrive at the clinic, where more Arise Africa kids are in the waiting room to be immunized. Isaiah sees a nurse, a doctor, an X-ray technician, and then the doctor again. The good news is that he's okay. The bad news is that the wound needs to be thoroughly cleaned. Dr. Michael keeps squeezing the wound together and letting it bounce back. I tap out and count on Lara and Joseph to step up. Isaiah would like to murder the doctor. At this point, I would too. *Can I get some morphine for us both over here?*

At 1:15 we get into another cab to head back to Isaiah's neighborhood. He is irritated with us all. A cotton candy–flavored Dum Dum doesn't help. Neither does the fact that the taxi smells like Fritos and that Zambian Acoustic Sunrise is blaring from all the speakers.

Joseph receives a call from Chris, asking for a favor. Could we run by Ms. Kaliki's to give her a message?

Running by Ms. Kaliki's is more of a drive-by. She lives on the streets just outside the lumberyard. Therefore, every minibus in the greater Zambian metropolitan area seems to be on her street. Joseph instructs the driver to start shouting "Kaliki" out the window when we get close. Ms. Kaliki's sister scrambles up and begins running alongside the car at a comfortable speed, and Joseph relays the message. Then Isaiah's grandmother starts waving to friends from the front seat because she's practically a celebrity riding around in a taxi. It's like she's the queen of a homecoming parade. A hot, sticky homecoming parade.

When we return Isaiah and his grandmother to their house, we give his mom the rundown on how she needs to treat Isaiah's leg. Then Joseph suggests we pray for the family. Isaiah's mom gently nudges him in our direction, and the kid . . . melts . . . down. He does *not* want to pray with white people who squeeze his open wound and then douse it with iodine. No, thank you. Lara prays anyway as Isaiah weeps tears of terror.

Hey, Jesus? Could you take that wheel again?

It's 2:00 in the afternoon, and we finally get back to Dotroda. You know, the place where Lara and I were supposed to work all day long. Chris, David, and Susan are cool. They don't have hard feelings about feeding one hundred kiddos by themselves. We decide the best plan of action is to buy a Coke from the stand next door and drown our sorrows in sugary goodness and beef jerky.

That's a game changer.

We discuss life, love, and how we can find Joseph a wife once he moves to Zimbabwe to go to the university. I have it all figured out. We're going to do an African version of *The Bachelor*, and it's going to be epic.

An hour later, we squish into a minibus headed for downtown. When we make the switch at the depot—for what reason, I'm unclear—Lara and I are escorted to the front seat with the driver while our friends giggle behind us. Joseph and Susan let the driver, Alfred, know we're looking for husbands, and he's all *game on!* He offers Lara fifteen cows and two minibuses as a dowry.

She's practically engaged! We take a selfie to celebrate.

At 3:45 we connect with our last bus. Susan's lap is violated this go-around by a lovely woman and her baby. I sit directly behind her. The conductor, Jimmy, gives me approximately twenty-three fist bumps in thirty minutes. How do I know his name is Jimmy? Because he gives me his phone number. It's not fifteen cows and two minibuses, but I still feel loved and accepted.

By the time Alissa picks us up at the bus stop corner and drives us back to the complex, it's 5:00. It feels like midnight.

Susan travels for two hours a day to get to Dotroda school. Chris is intentional with discipling every child at that same school. Joseph took an entire day out of his schedule to help Isaiah.

It's important to know that Isaiah isn't even sponsored by Arise Africa. He doesn't even go to the school. He's just a seven-year-old in the community who had a need. Arise Africa stepped in and did something about it.

It was a privilege to walk in each of their shoes. I learned that loving someone well means serving that person well too. I had no idea the lesson would hit home in a major way later that year.

9

Johnny Ray's Daughter

For those of us who look up to someone we **LOVE**

My dad is an intimidating man. He always has been. Since he wasn't much of a talker, he showed us how he felt through actions. Daddy demonstrated his love by providing for the family, no matter what it cost. The cost was never money. It was time.

The restaurant business is a seven-days-a-week and nearly twenty-four-hour-a-day commitment. We never went on vacation ourselves because Daddy opted for his employees to take time off to be with their families instead. When we were younger, we spent most weekends at the restaurant. Jamie and I played on the broken cash register in the stockroom for hours, read a few *Archie* comic books, and then wiggled into our sleeping bags we rolled out on the shelf that held the toilet paper. We'd fall fast asleep until the Friday night rush was over—or until someone came barging in to replenish the ketchup.

All holidays were spent at the restaurant. The four of us ran the place by ourselves. Jamie and Mama took care of the customers out front, and Daddy and I fried the catfish and made the coleslaw in the back. The days were busy enough for it to be worth our time, but slow enough that Daddy could enjoy the Cowboys game on the tiny orange Panasonic TV perched temporarily on top of the freezer.

I once questioned Daddy about how he absolutely violated all sorts of child labor laws, forcing his daughters to chop onions and take orders for an entire twelve-hour shift. He keenly noted that he would have given us a paycheck if we had been smart enough to ask for one.

Do you hear that, ten-year-old self? Demand wages when you're forced to spend Thanksgiving in a hot kitchen with nothing but your books to keep you company.

When we were old enough to figure out that we needed money to have a social life, Daddy made us work at the restaurant for pay instead of giving us an allowance. You haven't experienced true restraint until you've had someone throw a container of tartar sauce back at you through a drive-through window because it wasn't filled to the rim. Lovely.

Working with my dad never bothered me like it bothered my sister. That was probably because I was a complete angel who never did anything wrong compared to Jamie, who was known to be a hellion at times. (That delightful attribute is a direct quote from my mother.) Jamie never did anything horrific; we just had strict parents. As a result, she spent most of her freshman year grounded. At one point, my parents removed her bedroom door, so she couldn't slam it in frustration.

They soon realized my sister couldn't care less about being sent to her room, even if she didn't have a door or a phone. One day, when she pushed Daddy a little too far, he announced that she was too old to be grounded. Instead, she would go to work with him as punishment for her transgressions.

Worst idea *ever*.

Again, I never experienced this torture device because I was practically perfect in every way. I also had Jamie as a wonderful guide for what not to do to avoid crossing our parents. I just had to watch, listen, and learn from her mistakes. She was a superb guinea pig.

Today, Jamie is one of the most dedicated and accomplished individuals I know. Her work ethic is a direct result of her spending so much time with our father during her most formative years. We both watched him get up early, work tirelessly, come home late, and do it all again the next day. Year after year, he put in the hours and chose to miss recitals, prom nights, and award ceremonies because his job was making sure we had the opportunity to take dance lessons, wear beautiful sequined dresses, and attend our favorite colleges. Although he was rarely there in person, he was always there in spirit.

On the uncommon occasion he wasn't at work, the man was outside doing something. He never met a match, can of gasoline, or blade of grass he didn't want to strike, burn, or cut. He could fix anything, which was handy, because he broke most things he touched.

The house had a different vibe when Daddy was home. It felt complete.

Daddy shows love in abstract ways. You have to watch for it. The man speaks to his cattle and horses in sweet tones. I've seen him converse with his dog when no one was looking, warning him not to attack the ducks. When my niece was born, Jamie and I often stared at the strange man who cooed and bounced her baby with such intense adoration.

Where had that personality been hiding?

When his father passed away, I saw Daddy bow his head and silently weep as a member of the United States Army extended an exquisitely folded American flag, thanking Daddy for Papaw's time served, defending our country. It was the first and last time I have seen him cry.

He calls my friend Julie "Downtown Julie Brown." It's a weird term of endearment, but it's his way of telling her she's loved.

My friends Jill and Rebecca started visiting Hallsville about a decade ago. My parents became secondary grandparents to their broods of children. When we couldn't find the babies, we figured Daddy had snuck away with one or two of them, so he could drive them around the pond on his John Deere tractor.

When he turned seventy years old, I asked several friends and family members to send me a few words they thought described Daddy. The response was so overwhelming, I opted out of my original plan to write him a letter and instead built a word cloud using all the adjectives.

Strong, confident, steadfast, dedicated, hard-working, and *committed* made the cut. So did "raised eyebrow." *Brother, son, father, husband, Big Daddy,* and *friend* were mixed in too. We framed the piece of art and presented it to him with a huge slice of German chocolate cake. I could tell he was trying not to be overwhelmed, but I wanted him to know he's deeply loved by all who know him.

That's why I now secretly long for time to first rewind and then stand still. For just a little while.

You see, I'm not handling this new normal well, this current season of darkness, when I patiently listen as he tells me a story he told me moments ago.

I long to go back to the summer he surprised us with a trampoline or the time he drove home in a new ice-blue Cadillac for Mama. I'd watch him dig post holes, feed his horses, count cows, and read the *Longview News Journal* from front to back. I'd listen more when he spoke, knowing that if he's taking the time to talk, what he's saying must be educational or witty. And I would follow him around the restaurant, asking questions about building a business and how he kept it afloat for decades.

I would cherish the envelopes he sent me when I was at college. They held gas money paperclipped to a ripped-off piece of cash register tape, signed "Love, JR." The unspoken words "come see me" sprawled in bold, black letters. I would take a picture of him cuddling Jill's baby as though he were his own. I would record my niece's giggles when Daddy called her favorite cartoon character SpongeBob Square*Britches*.

My love for Daddy has evolved. It's changed its shape, but it remains a love story all the same. While I've still got him, I want him to know that his face comes to mind when I think of strength. I want him to know I'm so incredibly thankful for everything he's given me over the years, all the sacrifices he made to make my dreams a reality.

I will follow him around the yard and help him pick up sticks. I will smile as he talks to the dog in a baby voice. I will answer when he calls me Slink.

And I will tell him how much I love him, again and again and again.

10

Two Crazy Kids

For those of us who have learned to **LOVE** *a different way*

When I want to take in a real-life romantic love story, I look no further than my wonderful parents. Mama and Daddy have been married for almost fifty years, and no one could be more surprised than they are.

Yes, that sounds like an awful thing to say about the people who raised me, but when I asked Mama if she knew she and Daddy were meant to be, she threw back her head and laughed, refreshed her beverage of choice, and launched into the dramatic story of the day her life changed when she met Johnny Ray.

Get comfortable. Allow me to transport you to a simpler time. Back to yesteryear, when Friday night dates were as plentiful as the endless high-heeled shoes in my mother's closet. The year was 1969. The place was Dallas, Texas.

This is Mama's account of how Cupid shot his arrow that fateful afternoon.

Mama: "I was Johnny's second choice. It's the truth. The girl he came to see in another department already had a date that night. Johnny's friend said, 'I know another one up the hall. Let's ask her.'"

Daddy: [laughing]

Mama: "That's a polite way of saying, 'She'll do. She doesn't get out much.' To my credit, I didn't know I was second choice to a tall blonde. He likes to remind me all the time."

Daddy: [still laughing]

Mama: "I was a secretary working at . . ."

Daddy: "Monfield Industries."

Mama: "Right! And I don't know how Johnny got into the building, because you had to have an official badge. We made bombs, you know."

Lincee: "I'm sorry, what? You made bombs? What do you mean, 'We made bombs'?" [followed by a peal of laughter that lasted thirty seconds].

Mama: "We made casing for the big bombs that go on the huge jets when you go to war."

Lincee: "Aha. Granted, you weren't making actual bombs, but it was an important job nonetheless. Who knew that was going on in Dallas?"

Mama: "I was probably supposed to keep that a secret. Anyway, when I went home that day, after your daddy asked me out, my friend Gwen—"

Lincee: "Did she build bombs like you?"

Mama: "No. I can't remember what she did. We were getting ready because she had a date too."

Lincee: "Wow. Two women going on two dates in one night. With men. Men who pursued you and asked you to accompany them on a night on the town. What's that like?"

Mama: "Huh?"

Lincee: "Never mind."

Mama: "We both had dates and were both nervous because it was Friday the thirteenth. We figured it was going to be a doozy!"

Lincee: "Ha! No bad luck for you! What did you wear?"

Mama: "I don't know."

Daddy: "A mini dress."

Lincee: "Show that thigh, Mama! What did Daddy wear?"

Mama: "I know he didn't wear blue jeans." [makes a face]

Lincee: "Well of course not. He's not a heathen. Where did y'all go on your date?"

Mama: "This is when the story gets sticky."

Lincee: "Is it bad? Can I write about it in the book?"

Mama: "I don't know if I want you to write this down, because it's the first time I ever smelled marijuana."

[Cue Lincee falling to the ground in a heap, laughing her head off. Five minutes later, we continue.]

Mama: "We went over to The Cellar in Fort Worth, which doesn't make a lick of sense because it was on the second floor of a building. It should have been called The Attic, you know? Anyway, I said to your daddy, 'What is that smell?'"

Daddy: "It was weed."

Mama: "And I said, 'Are you smoking it?' And he said, 'No!'"

Daddy: [laughing]

Mama: "Please write in there that we did not smoke that stuff. No, no, no we did not. Johnny was on his best behavior."

Daddy: "We had a good time."

Mama: "We were married five months later. My mother said I married on the rebound. Is that ugly to admit?"

Daddy: "Nah. You were my second choice."

Lincee: "How long did you date before Daddy asked you to marry him?"

Mama: "One month."

Daddy: "I asked her, and she said yes. She had a washrag on her head."

Lincee: "Huh. A washrag, you say? This sounds interesting."

Mama: "Well, I wore a wig, and I had to get some height on it like Jacqueline Kennedy. So I put a washrag on top of my head and then put on my wig."

Daddy: "Then I did this." [Daddy gestures with his arms]

Mama: "Johnny spun me around on the dance floor in this fabulous move. He's such a good dancer—"

Daddy: "And I ended up with her wig in my hand."

Mama: "I was embarrassed at first, but then we laughed it off. I should tell you that his family thanked me over and over. They appreciated me marrying their son."
Daddy: "That's true."

Many look at them and see an unlikely pair. Daddy is an intro-vert who managed his own catfish restaurant for many decades. He likes burn piles and mud, mowing already mowed grass, and working cattle in remote fields. Johnny Ray is a loner.

Mama is an extrovert who taught school for many years. She likes to have lunch with her core group of friends, decorate the house with beautiful antiques, and work with her hands in the flower beds. Linea Ray is a nurturer.

He is forever dirty and rough around the edges. She is immacu-lately dressed and always ready for a good time. Before he even knows he's hungry, she's there with a pork chop, baked potato, and a chocolate pie she made from scratch. He's quiet. She's not. He's impatient. She's carefree. He barely smiles. Her smile lights up a room. He rarely talks. She holds marathon phone conversa-tions daily.

They don't look like they go together, but he's the yin to her yang. This union had to be ordained. It's the only explanation.

God knew what He was doing when He led Johnny Ray to Monfield Industries and down the hall to Linea Dorsey on June 13, 1969. He knew the love this man felt for this woman would transcend the test of time.

But when you love someone for better or for worse, you adapt. And adapt. On a weekly basis. On a daily basis. Sometimes you make the sacrifices hourly.

Change can be gut-wrenching. Mama and Daddy have good days and bad days, but one thing always remains the same: my parents' love for each other is strong. That love God knew would transcend the test of time has been tested, and it's still strong despite the fire.

Mama's got this. This new normal.

She's still the picture of grace and fortitude. She dotes on her husband, provides for him, and encourages him every step of the way. She never worries, because she has complete trust in the Lord. The woman doesn't stop. She's embraced this next chapter of their story with everything she's got, and she forges ahead one day at a time, with Daddy at her side.

11

"If You're a Bird, I'm a Bird"

*For those of us who want Hollywood to
make good* **LOVE** *stories again*

I believe we're in a romance/romantic comedy movie drought,
and we have been for many years. I long for the days of watching Sandra Bullock's high jinks while someone is sleeping.
Who wouldn't want to see Julia Roberts try to sabotage her
best friend's wedding? Why can't I cheer for Harry to realize
that Sally is the last person he wants to talk to before he goes
to sleep at night?

I've written about this horrific phenomenon on my blog and
waded through the comment section shouting *Amen, sister!*
when readers lament my exact frustrations. Many of them, and
I mean many of them, have strong feelings about romantic movies. I have never received so many comments, emails, texts, and
phone calls as I did with my love story podcast.

Should we all seek therapeutic intervention? Not necessarily. The way my readers compassionately defended a tiny little

movie called *Titanic* and Stella getting her groove back makes me smile. And it makes me a little scared.

Much as I blame Walt Disney with his princess fairy tales of love and marriage, I blame Nicholas Sparks for putting those same sentiments in a modern-day format.

I understand that diving into a Sparks movie means I must prepare myself for one of the main characters to perish. Also, an old person will impart wisdom, our leading characters will have some sort of revelation in the rain, and only ridiculously hot actors were considered for this adaptation of the book. Bring it on.

I think most movies today are all about CGI villains, blood, death, war, car chases, more death, brooding, guns, and secret societies of bad guys. Would you like to go see a movie about a time machine that's also a hot tub? No problem. May I offer you a creepy doll or scary clown holding a balloon? Take your pick. Hey, let's all go to the one where you sit in silence waiting for the monster to jump out and eat you. Good times.

Where did the romance go? Why did the epic love story fall off the writer's vision board in favor of murder, sex, and scandalous acts of betrayal? Do we all agree that Hollywood needs to do something about this huge gap in modern-day affairs of the heart?

Love stories teach us so much. I've gleaned a multitude of helpful hints simply by watching Meg Ryan get mail. How can we deny future generations the lessons we learned from the good old days?

Dirty Dancing—1987

I was twelve years old when *Dirty Dancing* debuted. Clearly, Mama saw the word *dirty* in the title of this movie I thought I had to see and decided it wasn't fit for a young girl.

LESSONS LEARNED FROM
Dirty Dancing:

→ Ignore all signage that reads "No guests allowed."

→ Carry watermelons. It might lead to great things.

→ You will never be as skinny as Penny. It's time to accept that fact.

→ When Patrick Swayze finger-wags for you to come here, you go there. Every time.

→ Warning: Pelvic thrusting can look awkward. Proceed with caution.

→ Make sure to have a talent on standby. You never know when a fun opportunity will present itself. Additionally, always travel with a costume or any props you might need. Throw a ukulele and a Hawaiian-themed bikini in a bag and keep it in the trunk of your car. Be prepared.

→ Fruit of the Loom bra and panties can be substituted for a leotard when you're in a pinch.

→ Wear a billowy skirt in case you're asked to perform the end-of-the-season showcase dance.

→ Travel with music. Preferably vinyl—45s.

→ The best place to practice lifts is in the water.

Jamie saw the movie about fifty-eight times and would come home and brag about the seductive music, the killer choreography, and the beauty of Patrick Swayze. Little did she know I'd

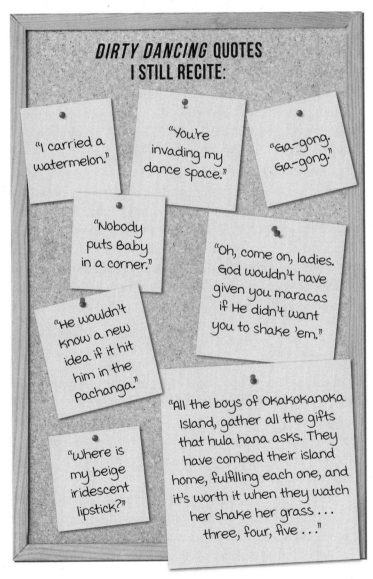

DIRTY DANCING QUOTES I STILL RECITE:

"I carried a watermelon."

"You're invading my dance space."

"Ga-gong. Ga-gong."

"Nobody puts Baby in a corner."

"Oh, come on, ladies. God wouldn't have given you maracas if He didn't want you to shake 'em."

"He wouldn't know a new idea if it hit him in the Pachanga."

"All the boys of Okakokanoka Island, gather all the gifts that hula hana asks. They have combed their island home, fulfilling each one, and it's worth it when they watch her shake her grass . . . three, four, five . . ."

"Where is my beige iridescent lipstick?"

95

attend Tiffany Tutt's birthday party later that year and that we'd watch the entire movie four times on a BETA tape.

I must tell you, I was hooked. It was a pivotal movie for me. Sure, there was a ton of sexually charged stuff, but I saw only the dancing, heard only the music, and gawked only at Johnny Castle. Later I would try to figure out ways to sit in a corner, longing for a tall, handsome fella dressed in black from head to toe to come and proclaim that nobody puts me in a corner.

You know you did that too. Admit it.

I loved when Penny and Johnny danced. I loved when Johnny bit his lower lip and gave Baby the "come here" gesture with his finger when they first met, after she carried a watermelon. Then he proceeded to lovingly teach her how to dance, well, dirtily. I envisioned myself in the "Hungry Eyes" montage. I know for a fact that I would not have laughed when Johnny tickled my armpit. *The man is topless. Don't be immature, Baby.*

A few years ago, *Dirty Dancing* commemorated its thirtieth anniversary (say it ain't so), and I saw the film in the movie theater. My sister was right. Nothing is like Johnny Castle twenty-two feet up in the air.

Clueless—1995

From the moment Cher Horowitz graced the big screen in her plaid outfit, I was mesmerized. This fashionista and her BFF Dionne had it all. As a girl from a town where you can drive from one end to the other in five minutes, I soaked up every ounce of this movie as though it were my own personal glimpse inside a cool person's world.

During my senior year at Baylor University, my Film/Media professor discussed an assignment that would be a big part of our semester grade. All we had to do was choose a classic movie and explain how it had woven itself into the tapestry of our culture.

LESSONS LEARNED FROM *Clueless:*

→ Helping people is fulfilling work.

→ Be aware of stumbling into bad lighting while on a date.

→ Paul Rudd is as timeless as the movie.

→ Blaming an "evil male" is a great excuse for almost anything.

→ It doesn't say RSVP on the Statue of Liberty.

→ Mexico and El Salvador are not the same place.

→ Hamlet did not say "To thine own self be true."

→ Billie Holiday is a woman.

My fellow students began buzzing with dibs on famous titles, such as *The Godfather* and *The Graduate*. Two girls fought over *Casablanca*. For a hot second I considered *Star Wars*, *Dazed and Confused*, or *Grease*.

When push came to shove, though, I chose *Clueless*.

Hello. *Clueless* was totally a cinematic legend—as long as one overlooked the fact that it had been out for only three years. All I had to do was take a drive down sorority row to see the film's effects on my generation's vernacular and wardrobe. I effortlessly wrote my paper, explaining how the kids in America were more independent, tech savvy, and health conscious because of that movie. Most long for comfortable knee socks and a good pair of purple clogs. I had precise points with clear examples.

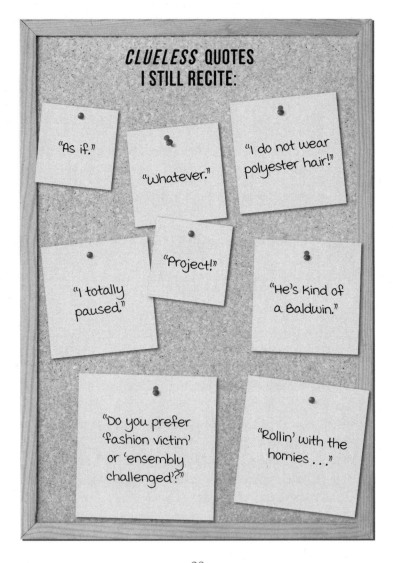

CLUELESS QUOTES I STILL RECITE:

"As if."

"Whatever."

"I do not wear polyester hair!"

"Project!"

"I totally paused."

"He's kind of a Baldwin."

"Do you prefer 'fashion victim' or 'ensembly challenged'?"

"Rollin' with the homies . . ."

Additionally, the movie introduced me to Paul Rudd, and I will forever be grateful.

I received an A on the paper. The professor read it out loud to the class, praising me for my remarkable work.

Okay, so he didn't really praise me. He sort of chastised me for not following the assignment, but he still thought it was important to grade me on my unique perspective. He admitted that *Clueless* had left its mark on the student body, but he highly doubted it would stand the test of time.

As if!

The Holiday—2006

In a list that spans the length of my arm, one of the staple "must-see" Christmas flicks I pull out every year is *The Holiday*. The movie boasts a stellar cast of characters. Kate Winslet can rarely do wrong in my book, Jack Black is just the right amount of cheese, Cameron Diaz is just the right amount of dork, and Jude Law is definitely the right amount of hotness.

Full disclosure: I didn't love *The Holiday* when I first saw it.

For those of you silently shunning me right now, take a breath and hear me out. The year 2006 was a sketchy time for me. I was in what friends call "the dark place." When I saw *The Holiday* for the first time, I completely related to Iris and her plight, trying to forget the man she loved who was going to marry someone else. Even Jude Law's spectacled baby blues couldn't break through the layer of sadness I associated with the film.

A few Decembers ago my sister pulled up the film on her newfangled, fancy-pants Apple TV. I sat poised with my hot chocolate as the sweat began to collect under my red-and-white snowflake pajamas. I was too embarrassed to tell Jamie this movie made me want to curl into the fetal position in my bed and eat fig Newtons.

LESSONS LEARNED FROM The Holiday:

→ Jerks populate this world. Don't be one of them.

→ Never hang out on someone's back burner.

→ The cure to loneliness during the holidays is participating in an overseas home exchange. You'll end up staying in either an adorable cottage or tricked-out crib, meet the love of your life, and live happily ever after.

→ Santa Ana winds are bewitching. Stand and wait for something to blow into your eye. A chivalrous stranger will waltz up and offer to remove it for you. You'll fight your feelings at first, but then fall hopelessly in love.

→ Always allow drunken strangers into your holiday home exchange cottage. Especially when they look like Jude Law.

→ It would be a good idea to write to Jude Law and ask him to create a YouTube tutorial that teaches men how to kiss.

→ Glasses make you look smarter. Or in Jude's case, smarter and hotter.

→ Befriend more old but spry Jewish men.

→ If a man writes a melody just for you, using only the good notes, explore that business.

→ Froodle-dee-do is a word.

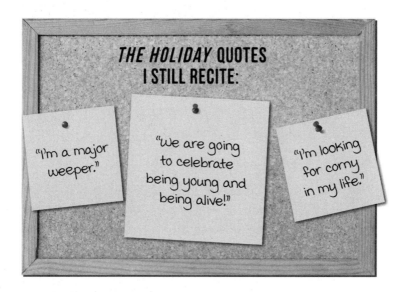

**THE HOLIDAY QUOTES
I STILL RECITE:**

"I'm a major weeper."

"We are going to celebrate being young and being alive!"

"I'm looking for corny in my life."

I'm glad I gave *The Holiday* a second chance. I saw the movie through a new set of eyes. Instead of identifying with the sad parts of the story line, I chose to dive headfirst into the relentless theme of hope. And the idea of loving again. And Jude Law entertaining his adorable daughters as Mr. Napkinhead.

My Best Friend's Wedding—1997

I have a confession to make. I've always felt a little guilty for sort of understanding why Jules wants to steal Michael back from Kimmy. I completely blame this movie for my belief that "if you love someone, you say it, right then, out loud."

Or write it in a poem. Or say it through the power of a mixtape.

Dermot Mulroney is so handsome in a chiseled sunglasses model sort of way. Although I don't condone Julia Roberts's position as "the bad guy," I can see why she's in a panic with only four days to break up a wedding and steal the bride's fella. I'd secretly

101

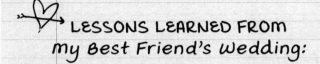

LESSONS LEARNED FROM My Best Friend's Wedding:

→ Julia Roberts's hair can never be replicated. Nor can her smile. We should all stop trying.

→ Yes, you can be chartreuse with envy.

→ The best place to have an intervention is in an elevator after the emergency stop button has been pressed.

→ Have a karaoke song list on standby. May I suggest "Sin Wagon," or "Sweet Caroline."

→ Even if your singing is horrible, take heart. Your one true love will find your tone deafness and lack of harmony delightful.

→ Diabolical plans purposed to screw up weddings seldom work out.

→ Tell the guy you love him. Even if you expect your heart to be crushed.

→ Never, ever try on another woman's wedding.

→ Be careful around gazebos. Really good things might happen there, but really embarrassing things can happen there too.

→ Only kiss the groom if you're the bride.

→ Always have a song you consider "yours."

→ Maybe there won't be marriage, but *there will be dancing.*

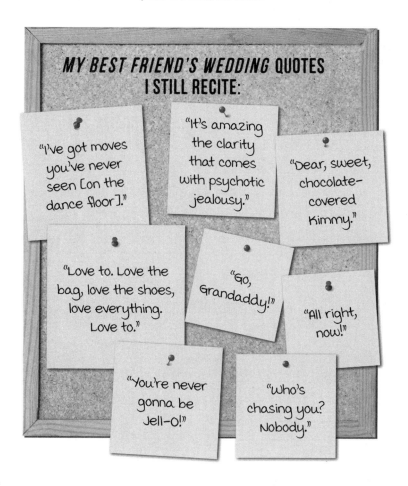

MY BEST FRIEND'S WEDDING QUOTES I STILL RECITE:

"I've got moves you've never seen [on the dance floor]."

"It's amazing the clarity that comes with psychotic jealousy."

"Dear, sweet, chocolate-covered Kimmy."

"Love to. Love the bag, love the shoes, love everything. Love to."

"Go, Grandaddy!"

"All right, now!"

"You're never gonna be Jell-O!"

"Who's chasing you? Nobody."

root for our leading characters to recognize the love that's been right in front of them for the last nine years if Cameron Diaz wasn't so adoringly charming. You go, Kimmy, with your brightly colored dresses and pastel cardigans. Clutch those pearls, girl!

While You Were Sleeping—1995

I think we can all agree that even though Sandra Bullock was our glimmer of hope for a love story in the blockbuster action

LESSONS LEARNED FROM
While You Were Sleeping:

→ Don't jump onto the train tracks to save someone, unless that person looks exactly like or is more attractive than Peter Callahan.

→ Pretending to be someone's fiancée is totally fine if that person is in a coma and is literally unable to counter your lie.

→ Hospitals are full of three things: ice chips, germs, and secrets.

→ Never play basketball with a pencil in your pocket.

→ Beware of the ruggedly handsome brother.

→ White carpet is begging to have something spilled on it.

→ If Jack Callahan and Noah Calhoun taught us anything, it's to date someone who can build furniture.

→ Carry your passport at all times.

→ Slipping on ice can be romantic.

→ Leaning is a lot different from hugging.

→ Pay attention to the lonely people.

→ Train token booths don't seem like the perfect place to propose, but they work.

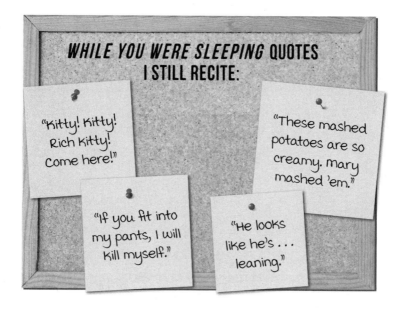

WHILE YOU WERE SLEEPING QUOTES I STILL RECITE:

"Kitty! Kitty! Rich Kitty! Come here!"

"These mashed potatoes are so creamy. Mary mashed 'em."

"If you fit into my pants, I will kill myself."

"He looks like he's . . . leaning."

flick *Speed*, she really shone her brightest in the love triangle classic *While You Were Sleeping*. There's a sweetness about this romance. From the moment Lucy admitted she had fallen for someone from a distance, we all related.

Let's just ignore that part where she dips her Oreo into the cat's milk dish.

The Bodyguard—1992

The few months of summer before my senior year in high school were glorious, a precious time when the thought of filling out college applications was easily ignored by more urgent needs— like lying in the sun without getting tan lines and deciding at whose house we would watch *Seinfeld* reruns.

I went to drill team camp every summer, and that year our instructors wisely decided our entire catalog of routines would be choreographed to the powerful vocal stylings and rhythmic magic of *The Bodyguard* soundtrack. If I listen hard enough, I can still make out the squeals of delight upon hearing the opening cadence of the "Queen of the Night" pep rally dance.

We also learned a lyrical dance to "I Have Nothing" (one I can still perform to this day) and a contemporary piece to "I'm Every Woman." We sang "I Will Always Love You" at the top of our lungs at the end of the night, because we were teenage girls powered by Cheese Nips, M&Ms, grape Fanta, and funky choreography.

LESSONS LEARNED FROM THE BODYGUARD:

→ A man who scoops up a woman in a crowd when she's being assaulted by her adoring fans is attractive.

→ A man who fights a thug without saying a single word is attractive.

→ Drinking straight orange juice is attractive.

→ A man who knows how to handle a gun is attractive.

→ A man who takes you to a dive bar and slow dances with you is attractive.

→ A man who jumps into freezing cold water to save your child is attractive.

→ A man who jumps in front of a bullet to save your life is attractive.

Whitney Houston commanded this role that helped catapult her into stardom. And she did it by letting Kevin Costner guard her body all the livelong day. I wasn't the only one who imagined myself in Whitney's position. This is '90s Kevin Costner we're talking about. The guy who liked to play baseball in cornfields and dance with wolves and steal money from the rich to give to the poor. If given the opportunity, you would absolutely let him guard your body and fall in love with you while doing it. No questions asked.

Whether in a moment of inspiration you suddenly realize you love your stepbrother Josh or you fall in love with the other brother while the first one is sleeping, I'm here for you. I will applaud you and your bad boy beau during the final dance of the season, and I will help you pack up your mansion, so you can move across the ocean to be with your beloved.

I will always root for you. And I will always root for love.

12

Fake Vision of Love

For those of us who fantasize about **LOVE**

I will root for you all day long, but I'll understand if the gesture isn't reciprocated. After all, I'm one who, shall we say, lives with her head in the clouds when it comes to love, and whose steady beaus aren't viable options.

When the bored nurse dressed in scrubs passes me paperwork at the doctor's office and insists I check my relationship status, I typically draw an additional box under "single," "married," or "divorced" to include "mentally dating a fictional character."

Through the years, I have courted a multitude of men from both the big and small screen. The list is lengthy, and to be perfectly honest, it's been culled. There's no need for you to urgently call or text my loved ones. I understand I have a problem.

Instead of writing an ode to each of my hypothetical sweethearts, I've taken the liberty of simply explaining why I knew I could marry any one of them if he were an actual human being.

This is where I choose to live. Raise a glass, and let's make a toast to Lincee's imaginary boyfriends. Cheers!

Jake Ryan from *Sixteen Candles*

Like most forward-thinking girls, I thought if I only met Jake, he would fall in love with me and ask me to be his girlfriend the afternoon after my birthday. All I had to do was get my sister to her own wedding and make sure she was blitzed enough to forget her veil in the chapel. That way, when I went to the sanctuary to retrieve it, I could watch an old clunky car drive in the direction of the reception, revealing a red Porsche with my dearest Jake leaning against it. He would wave. I would look confused, because why is hotter-than-crap Jake Ryan waving at me? I'd point to myself in unmitigated disbelief, and he would chuckle and say, "Yeah, you." Best birthday ever.

Oliver Queen from *Arrow*

Oliver Queen may not be a man of many words, but he can wield a bow and arrow like it's his job, which it is 90 percent of the time. All he wants to do is rid Star City of villains while wearing a green leather hooded suit and black mask. One must be in tip-top shape to fend off bands of thugs setting up shop in the ship channel. I would be willing to encourage him, and maybe video all workout sessions, especially when he's dominating the salmon ladder. Google it.

Pacey Witter from *Dawson's Creek*

I'm the loyal fan who may have written a strongly worded letter to the WB Network on my personalized Precious Moments stationery, asking someone in charge to please explain to me why this cult classic wasn't titled *Pacey's Creek*. Pacey was by far the best part of the show. He was romantic and not afraid to be emotional, because he was secure in his manliness. I pictured him holding my hand, touching his forehead to mine, and professing his love for me in public, using props and passionate tirades. I also visualized what it would be like to spend the summer with him on his boat, even though I knew my mom would never let me voyage around the world with a boy while I was in high school. Luckily, she can't infiltrate my imagination. *Sail away, Lincee!*

Tristan Ludlow from *Legends of the Fall*

I'm pretty sure all it would take for me to fall in love with Tristan is for him to flash me that megawatt smile and flick water off his hat when he meets me. It happened through the movie screen, and I'm sure it could happen in real life.

Randall Pearson from *This Is Us*

I'd be willing to bet that I'm not the only one out there who's proclaimed out loud that I would prefer a marriage like Beth Pearson has with Randall. Tell me I'm wrong.

Rolfe from *The Sound of Music*

Y'all. A boy secretly meeting me in a gazebo? Please and thank you. I will merrily cavort and leap up onto benches during a thunderstorm. I will sing and dance with him all night long. I thought Rolfe was a fox. But then Jamie explained that it was inappropriate for me to crush on him because he supported Nazi Germany. What a wretched day. Being forced to choose one of the von Trapp boys as a backup didn't make the darkness any lighter. As if Friedrich or Kurt could hold a candle to Rolfe's charisma.

Wade Kinsella from *Hart of Dixie*

Maybe it's my East Texas roots, but I was drawn to Wade Kinsella like an Alabama tourist is drawn to the Rammer Jammer. I like the way he gives everyone a nickname, and I've speculated what my pet name would be more times than I care to admit. I landed on "darlin'"—"darling" without the "g." He owns a bar, a truck, and a guitar, and he rarely wears a shirt. Quadruple threat, my friends.

King T'Challa from *Black Panther*

Is he royalty? Yes, but that's only partially what makes T'Challa great. The other pieces of the pie include his killer good looks, his confidence, his combat abilities, and his willingness to let me fight the rotten aliens right alongside him in battle. I do love a man dressed in black. Also, my sister-in-law would be Shuri, and I would live in Wakanda. Done.

Noah Calhoun from *The Notebook*

My love for Noah Calhoun is well documented. If any fictional man could reach the pinnacle of my personal fake boyfriend Mount Everest, it's this guy. Noah is passionate, steadfast, a handyman, and lives to love others well. The moment he captured my soul was when he looked longingly at Allie and asked her a simple question: "You wanna dance with me?" This is my everything. If I was on death row, I would exchange my last meal of cheese pizza from Dominos with a side of ranch dressing for swaying to the melody of an extremely romantic song in the middle of a deserted street with Noah Calhoun. Mic drop.

Since I have yet to find an actual guy who happens to be alive and knows how to make me laugh, this list will have to do. However, should anyone bump into Zachary Levi soon, please pass my contact information along. I think I may have an actual shot with him, because he's a living, breathing, self-proclaimed nerd who was the voice of the best Disney prince ever—Flynn Rider.

If we all work together, we can make this a reality. Teamwork makes the dream work.

13

'Tis the Season

For those of us who **LOVE**
a Hallmark Christmas movie

Every year women across the world prepare themselves for the onslaught of brand-new Hallmark Christmas movies. To play each one multiple times per week, the network executives made the controversial decision to begin airing holiday-themed original programming around the time the new school year begins.

Although this seems like a viable solution to help mothers not day-drink during the delicate autumn months, the real reason Hallmark hauls out the goods around Labor Day is simple: they need four months to also schedule all the previous year's made-for-TV yuletide love stories.

I'm exaggerating, but not by much.

More than a hundred Christmas-themed movies are associated with the Hallmark Channel each year (about a third of them new). That's a lot of Winnie Cooper, Gretchen Wieners, and D.J. Tanner.

Extensive details must be researched and calculated, and lists must be compiled, because there's just not enough time to see them all. And I'm not naive enough to think that each of the wannabe artistic masterpieces is worth my time. In junctures like these I turn to the person who can be my guiding light, the only one who can point me in the right direction.

That would be Mama.

She told me not to bother with the one about the plucky girl who's engaged to the man who wears a power suit, but ultimately learns the sweet guy in her life turns out to be her true love and they figure all this out in the days leading up to December 25.

Not helpful, Mother.

Come December, I'm forced by straight-up curiosity and an obsession with love stories to go all-in, embracing every magical small town in the middle of a winter wonderland, where the locals are all captivated by Christmas. I have every confidence I'll see a holiday festival of some sort, an old person who gives romantic advice, and a twist that makes the viewer nervous about whether the two leads will end up together.

Of course, we'd never buy that. He will leave his legal practice in the city and move to Small Town, USA, so he can operate a tree farm (which is what he's always wanted to do), and where she owns a bakery that's about to be closed down because times are hard. She will always wear something either red or green, and she will always look fabulous.

Residents will be wearing Santa hats, serving coffee out of a little shack in the square. You know, the same town square where they hold the annual Christmas tree lighting.

If you or someone you know is from one of these small towns in the Midwest, whose townsfolk are consumed with all things Christmas, please contact me. I'd like to hear more about this phenomenon. I think I could be happy there.

My name is Lincee Ray, and I am not ashamed of my Hallmark Channel Christmas movie habit. I love this genre so much that I've developed an assortment of fan fiction that's both joyful and triumphant. Here are some thoughts and story ideas for future Christmas-y romances.

O Holey Night

Organizing the annual holiday world-record event is nothing for yarn store owner Belle. She knows the citizens of Prancer, Pennsylvania, will rise to the challenge of helping her knit the largest stocking in the history of the world by the Christmas Eve deadline. What Belle didn't expect was the infestation of hungry moths living in the town's gazebo. Thankfully, entomologist Robert just happens to be following the migration pattern of this swarm. Will he be able to save the world-record-breaking stocking from disintegrating before everyone's eyes? And can he crochet his way into the heart of a certain shop owner?

We Three Kings

Holly surprises her stockbroker boyfriend, Dexter, with a holiday getaway to an exclusive resort on Poinsettia Peak for an entire week. Unfortunately, Dexter's powerhouse job keeps him from leaving right away, and Holly is forced to enjoy Christmas merriment alone. Or is she? She meets Cash, a rugged cowboy, riding horses through the snowy banks. Then a doting doctor named Connor rescues her on the ice-skating rink by wrapping her sprained foot. Finally, high school teacher Caleb recommends a few books found in the resort library. Holly has no idea that Cash, Connor, and Caleb, who are brothers, are all there celebrating the King Family Christmas Reunion. Love triangles are so 2008. With whom in the love quadrangle will Holly roast chestnuts over an open fire? And which brother will Dexter attempt to punch in the mouth for scheming on his girlfriend?

What Child Is This?

Brave and attractive firefighter Travis Fuego never expected to find a baby boy abandoned on the steps of Station 24 the week of Christmas. Something else he didn't anticipate? His supermodel girlfriend, Jocelyn, threatening to leave him if he brought little Nick home to his posh apartment. For the first time in years, Travis leaves the bright lights of the big city for the slower-paced lifestyle of his hometown. His parents welcome him and the baby, no questions asked, back to Silver Bells Bluff. When a few hay bales from the town square's nativity accidentally catch fire, Travis's instincts kick in and he extinguishes the blaze. He's surprised to discover his old flame, Missy Tole, is the event coordinator for the nativity and is in desperate need of a baby Jesus. Will Missy forgive him for his past mistakes if he lets her borrow Nick for the manger?

All I Want for Christmas Is Hugh

Merry has watched the Christmas classic *Love Actually* a million times. Her best friend and bookshop owner, William, may poke fun at her obsession with Hugh Grant, but each year he watches the movie with her while eating figgy pudding. When Merry hears Hugh Grant's car broke down in Garland Falls the night before, she's determined to find her celebrity crush. Dozens of clues send her on a wild goose chase all around the tiny town. Hugh was seen applauding during the tree-lighting ceremony, admiring the Victorian-themed carolers, and enjoying a horse-drawn sleigh ride in the snow. She eventually ends up in William's store. Will he confess that Hugh Grant was in Garland Falls for a total of only twenty minutes? And the guy everyone has been confusing for Hugh Grant is him? Will he get the chance to tell Merry that he's just a boy, standing in front of a girl, asking her to love him at Christmastime?

Jingle Bell Rock

When adoring fans rip apart his lucky tour jacket, Jon and his bandmates make a pit stop in Snow Frost to mend it. Luckily, Ginger is the local seamstress and purveyor of the darling fashionable coats available to all women who live in or visit Snow Frost. Unfortunately, Ginger is unable to help match his worn faux leather since the only fabric choices in the entire tri-region area are limited to winter white, evergreen, Santa red, and ice-blue wools. Jon processes his emotions by playing an acoustic set of Christmas carols at the local orphanage. Will Ginger have enough time to convince the wise old butcher to skin a bovine, so she can make a new jacket out of the cowhide before Jon finishes his encore? Will Jon, a vegetarian, accept the precious gift?

Joy to the Worlds

When the Excelsis Deo Starship crashes on Earth, cyborg Joy springs into action. She infiltrates the tiny town of Wintergreen and adopts the locals' celebratory spirit while making gingerbread cottages at the mayor's house. When she reaches into a bowl of festive gumdrops, her metal hand grazes someone else's hand, but she has no idea because she can't feel a thing. She looks up and immediately falls in love with mechanic Dan. Will Dan give Joy the plutonium he's hiding in his auto shop to help generate the 1.21 gigawatts Joy needs to propel her back to her world? Or will Joy stay in Wintergreen, knowing she'll short-circuit every time Dan instigates an impromptu snowball fight in the middle of the street?

Brace Your Elves

Each advent season, the petulant rascals from the town of Bah Humbug have one goal: steal holiday cheer from the families in Star Bright. Rumor has it that this year they'll be vandalizing

Santa's Workshop. The hoodlums of Bah Humbug plan to substitute the cheerful elves with cheesy cutouts of Justin Bieber and Beyoncé. Angel and Aaron both volunteer to be on the Star Bright Task Force and are committed to guarding all of Santa's helpers. When Aaron starts humming "Sleigh my name, sleigh my name" under his breath, Angel realizes she no longer has to be ashamed of her Bieber Fever. Can they save the elves and snag a few cutouts for themselves when no one is looking? And will they fall in love when Aaron gets a nasty paper cut and Angel mends him with a Band-Aid?

Let It Go, Let It Go, Let It Go

Gloria is in a bind. The Sparkling Ridge Guild has voted for the community theater to perform a holiday adaptation of *Frozen* at the Candlelight Christmas Spectacular. There's just one problem: the show can't go on without a Sven, and Gloria's ex is the only reindeer rancher in town. Can she convince Kris to let her borrow a reindeer for the show? Even though the last reindeer Gloria borrowed ended up in a savory stew?

Brew Christmas

Carol Bernstein is a world-famous doctor from Seattle Grace Memorial who is in town to perform emergency brain surgery on her father. Carol is also Jewish and slightly annoyed by all the Santa hats no one seems to be wearing ironically. She breezes into Tag Goldberg's old-fashioned saloon to drown her sorrows. Will her spirits lift when she sees Tag's Star of David necklace and dreidel collection? Does Tag have the chutzpah to keep the bar open on December 25?

Don't be surprised if you see a sampling of these exceptional narratives on a Hallmark Channel near you this year. I expect my spritely work of art will debut around Halloween. I've polled several friends, and they're all on board with each scenario. Even though my mother claims there's no room for half-human, half-robots in her holiday-themed binge-watching sessions, I encourage you not to discriminate against bionic people or those individuals who may want a little science fiction in their yuletide romance.

And don't think for a minute that Queen Candace Cameron Bure isn't ready to stretch her acting wings beyond "time traveling turn of the century nurse" and "wacky twin sister." She would own that cyborg role like a boss.

14

Hangin' Tough

For those of us who will **LOVE** *them forever*

My treasured romantic comedies and fairy tales aren't the only outlet for my infatuation with love stories. I am a child of the '80s. We're a generation that appreciates beautifully scripted verses that describe all matters of the heart in great detail, no matter how embarrassing they may be to the performer or audience member.

Layer those heartfelt love letters over elegant melodies and you'll find me combing through junk drawers looking for a lighter. I'll need to pay proper tribute to the symphonic magnum opus enveloping all my senses at once with a solitary flame of respect.

Picture this:

I'm in the center section in the colossal venue, row twelve. In my opinion, I have the perfect viewpoint to allow New Kids on the Block to dance and sing their way further into my heart. I'm about to behold the wonder that is Jordan, Danny, Donnie,

Jonathan, and Joey in person for the first time ever, and I am absolutely beside myself.

I can identify Jordan's falsetto with my own ears. I can scrutinize the intricate microphone stand placement as it pertains to "Step By Step" choreography. And finally, I can settle the inner struggle my soul wrestles with every day of my life—trying to decide which New Kid is my favorite.

Do you see that girl? Will you channel her excitement? Can you feel her angst?

Now picture that girl as a thirty-six-year-old woman. The young me is rolling her eyes at the old me right now. I don't blame her.

I was minorly obsessed with New Kids on the Block as a tween. One day Keri Morgan came to school wearing her acid-washed denim jacket and showcasing the biggest vanity button I had ever seen pinned in the upper left quadrant.

Keri's love for New Kids was so genuine that she wore them over her heart for most of seventh grade.

Oh, don't get me wrong. I had buttons too. It was 1988, after all, and I was overtly aware of all the moderately questionable fashion trends. I embraced them with an enthusiasm as high as my bangs.

I had a button that said "I amaze myself," and another in the shape of a Mickey Mouse head. I also had a beautiful rhinestone pin that spelled out New York City.

I had never been to New York City, but that's not the point. What I'm saying is that my buttons were weak compared to the dinner plate protecting Keri's sternum.

Upon further inspection of said dinner plate, I was drawn to the delicate bone structure, boyish grin, and freshly permed hair of one Mr. Joseph Mulrey McIntyre. As Keri explained that Joey was a member of an all-boy band called New Kids on the Block, I quickly realized I was probably this guy's one true love and should get down to Sam Goody as fast as possible to buy my future husband's album.

If you consider this train of thought from a junior high perspective, it's on brand.

I never considered that Joey might be Keri's soul mate too. If anyone had dibs, Keri was definitely the one who deserved his hand in marriage because of her commitment to wear an accessory where Joey's face was the exact same ratio as her own.

I had a Joey button, but had I owned a button with Joey's face as big as mine, I would have kissed that face. Every single night. No question. I still feel good about this thought process.

I researched New Kids on the Block like I was studying for a final. Not only did I wear out my cassette tape, but I made sure to catalog every bit of news, information, and photo splashes from *Tiger Beat* into a useful collage.

Fun fact: "I'll Be Loving You Forever" was the theme of Hallsville Junior High's eighth grade dance. I slow swayed with Toby Mullikin for four minutes and twenty-three seconds as Jordan serenaded us. It was the best day ever.

When MTV infiltrated my adolescent world, the research project turned into a major deep dive. Life dramatically shifted that fateful summer.

I suffered "member guilt" as I witnessed the "Hangin' Tough" video for the first time. "Member guilt" is a medical term I invented and plan to trademark in the near future. This juvenile ailment produces frustrating and confusing emotions in a young girl's brain.

You see, I reveled in the vocal stylings of my boys and appreciated all their block had to offer, yet I had never seen them in action. Watching Joey bounce around in the background wearing his grandfather's fedora was exquisite. I wanted to pledge allegiance to him right then and there, to love him forever.

But I couldn't see beyond the dude in a pair of ripped jeans and black leather jacket owning the mic like a master front man/child/kid.

No ma'am, I told myself. Donnie was not for me, even though by the looks of his little brother, Marky Mark, my sister often projected that great genes ran in the family and Donnie probably had a lot going on in the physique department.

But he's a bad boy! I screamed in my own head. *He has an earring and some sort of rat-tail mullet situation. This cannot be good.* I spent the rest of junior high pretending to love Joey with my whole heart while secretly crushing on Donnie. My member guilt gave me heartburn. I'm confident it was my newfound disorder and not the pile of cheesy tatchos I'd eat for lunch.

Tatchos = tater tots plus nachos = tipping point!

Growing up, we never went to concerts. I believe the first musical event I attended where an employee took a ticket and I sat down to listen to someone share his or her music as I sang along was probably with Point of Grace in college.

I've been catching up ever since.

When the word got out that New Kids on the Block were touring again as grown men, I vowed to the world and everyone near my office cubicle that day that I would be going to the concert and no one could stop me.

Step one: Find my Joey button. My mother has been known to wear my old dancing leotards from the '90s as a bathing suit. Surely she still had my Joey button in the attic. Fingers crossed.

Step two: Find acid-washed jeans and a Home Boy T-shirt before event. Do not let me down, eBay.

Step three: Decide, finally, which of the five is my favorite New Kid.

My friends and I made our way to Toyota Center in downtown Houston, and I quickly became intoxicated by the anticipation of being transported back to my childhood.

And then the lights went out.

And the audience went crazy.

Did I mention that Boyz II Men was the opening act?! *Come on.* They were decked out in all white and kicked off their portion of the concert with the old classic "On Bended Knee." The stadium dwellers were on their feet, belting out every word of every song. I was right there with them, singing as loudly as I could. The Boyz were smooth, confident, and sounded just like they had coming from the speakers of my pink Jambox. Shawn Stockman took us to church numerous times. It was illustrious.

One can never prepare for the sheer adrenaline rush of "Motownphilly." Whatever you're imagining in your head right now, multiply it by ten, because you can't imagine the electricity that filled the space.

Hello again, 1991. I've missed you.

The guys bow to a standing-room-only crowd and then leave the stage, and an arena full of women tricked out on boy-band endorphins settle in their chairs so they can catch their breath.

In a matter of minutes, the lights begin to adjust, and I sway as the music swells to reveal four lone microphones standing on the stage. After my Boyz II Men high, I was quite confident that 98 Degrees would be hard-pressed to convince me to stand up.

I laugh thinking about the spastic twentysomething fan girl who was probably two sections up from me thinking, *Why are all the old ladies sitting down? Can they see Nick Lachey's biceps from there?*

Why is my example so specific? Because at a later concert (no judgment) when New Kids teamed up with the Backstreet Boys, a gaggle of ladies a generation younger than me barely flinched when Donnie ripped off his shirt during "Cover Girl." I'm standing on my chair screaming my lungs out. They're choosing an Instagram filter.

It took everything inside me not to knock their cell phones out of their social media–updating hands and demand that they *respect their elders* while lovingly yet firmly shaking them as I said, "Snap *this*, you fools!"

I also thought, *Huh. Jamie was right. It looks like Donnie has been using his brother Mark's old workout routine from his Calvin Klein modeling days!*

I'm much older now, which means I'm also able to dole out advice to those who may not have my street smarts. Perhaps I could educate the saplings on the symbolism of "Tonight" and the intricate workings of Jordan's torso. I did major in ab-ology. Isn't that the point of these bi-generational concerts? To bring us all together in the spirit of three-part harmony and pelvic thrusts?

Once 98 Degrees finished, the lights came up and a deejay began mixing songs from the late '80s and early '90s. I sang "I Wanna Dance with Somebody" to my friend Leslie and went to the extreme with Emmarie during "Ice Ice Baby." Lara agreed with Paula Abdul that opposites do attract, as Emily vogued her way to the concession stand.

I had a startling sensation that I needed to fetch the travel hairspray out of my purse to adjust my hair volume during "Livin' on a Prayer." Ah, Jon Bon Jovi. Thank goodness member guilt doesn't transfer from one musical group to another.

Suddenly the lights went out.

And the audience went crazy.

There they were. All five of them. No longer kids, but men. Singing a song I didn't know or care about but grew to love, and that I've since purchased on iTunes. Joey was on fire. Jordan was hotter than fire. Jonathan looked like he was about to hurl. Danny was just being Danny, and Donnie had on a pesky shirt.

"The Right Stuff" blew the roof off the building. I got tickled while singing and perfectly executing the now infamous dance moves, because at that exact same moment I realized the confusion I'd caused on Facebook earlier that day.

I had simply posted "Oh, oh, oh, oh, oh" just to see how many people would immediately comment in a jealous rage because they'd realized I had tickets to the hottest concert ever for people born from 1973 to 1983. Instead I got a lot of confusion about which song I was reciting—"Hangin' Tough" or "The Right Stuff." Based on which "oh" you emphasize, I can see why they were flustered.

Someone got rich thanks to those stellar, repeatable lyrics. This person is my hero.

And as though the traditional New Kids lineup wasn't enough, Joey busted out George Michael's "Faith," followed by Jordan's perfect rendition of Prince's "Kiss." Then we sang "Deep in the Heart of Texas."

I. Was. Slain.

For those of you who don't know, we Texans are proud of our heritage and have entire catalogs of songs dedicated to our grand state. We're big, we wear boots, we don't like to be messed with, and we'll tell you in a heartbeat that we can fly our flag the same height as the American one because we were once an independent nation.

The New Kids totally got us.

My loyalties shifted back and forth between Joey's charming personality and moving rendition of "Please Don't Go Girl" (now a few keys below the original recording), Jordan's mandate to be loving me forever (hopefully with those abs), and Donnie's bad boy persona. At the end of the concert, I decided to embrace all five kids.

Then I changed my mind. I chose Jordan, because he's a single kid on the block. This could work for me if I play my cards right. Of course, then I quickly claimed Joey again, because nostalgia will get you every time. Naturally, 1988 Donnie's grin flashed somewhere in the back of my eyeballs, and I asked Lara if she had any paper so I could begin drafting a pro/con list.

Member guilt. It's a real thing.

For an entire two hours, I celebrated a time before deadlines, schedules, heartache, and all the other responsibilities of adulthood. The lyrics are full of memories. The melodies are each a piece of my musical history. It may be a corny history, but it's mine. And these are the moments that give me perspective and keep me young.

15

The Soundtrack of My Life

For those of us who **LOVE** *a jukebox hero*

While shopping at Nordstrom recently, I overheard a young girl refer to Houston's local Lite-FM-Easy-Listening-Safe-For-Work radio station as the station that plays "oldies." I chuckled under my breath, completely judged the mother for not educating her daughter on the bedrock of great music. Then fought hard not to barricade the adolescent moppet inside the dressing room so I could educate her about today's pop music and how it's fundamentally impossible for me to believe that Ludacris and Pitbull can be featured in so many compilations.

I stopped myself, though. I've been down that lecture road before, and it never ended well. While standing in line at a grocery store, the song "True Colors" came on the radio, and this punk kid buying pepperoni Bagel Bites complained to his friend that "this old lady singer totally janked this song from that movie *Trolls*."

I beg your pardon?

I intervened immediately and rectified the situation right there in the express lane, while singing Cyndi Lauper's praises. They looked at me like I was a moron.

Much like I was exasperated by her bite-sized, pizza-loving comrades, with whom she shares a cohort, I was a touch annoyed by the way the darling whippersnapper in Nordstrom threw around the word *oldies* as if she knew what it really meant. I have an entire playlist on iTunes dedicated to oldies. It's full of Buddy Holly, Patsy Cline, Sam Cooke, and a ton of boy/girl groups that put *the* in front of an arbitrary noun: The Four Seasons, The Four Tops, The Dixie Cups, The Drifters, and The Ronettes.

I made my way back to my car and turned on Sunny 99 to see what was playing. Hello, Madonna! And I'm not talking about her random later works that make me concerned for her well-being. No, I'm talking about vintage "Open Your Heart" Madonna. I sang every word. I added a lot of personality to my rendition and felt pretty good about myself.

The deejay transitioned right into "Total Eclipse of the Heart." I was in heaven. Bonnie Tyler's raspy voice. The crescendos. And what's this? Poison! Why yes, I would like for you to give me something to believe in.

Just as Bret Michaels was about to do that little "huh" before the last chorus, a strange question crept into my subconscious. When did this song come out?

I need you to prepare yourself for this next part. It's going to be a tough read, but we'll get through it together. I promise.

A quick Google search slapped me in the face with these cold hard truths:

- "Something to Believe In" debuted in 1991. That was the year I started driving.
- Madonna's "Open Your Heart" came out in 1986. Ronald Reagan was president.

- Bonnie Tyler's "Total Eclipse of the Heart" debuted in 1983. A tank of gas cost ninety cents.
- Phil Collins's "Don't Lose My Number" was a top hit in 1985. In twenty-two years, we will no longer have to worry about misplaced numbers because everyone has them stored in smartphones.
- Sweet teen icon Tiffany bopped out to "I Think We're Alone Now" in 1987. At this writing she's forty-seven years old.
- Dexys Midnight Runners's "Come On Eileen" blasted my speakers in 1982. That was the year Brooke Shields sported those Calvin Kleins.
- The Boss's "Dancing in the Dark" hit air waves in 1984. Another five years, and Taylor Swift will be born.

Are you still vertical? Do you need a brown paper bag? Just breathe. In through the nose. Out through the mouth.

Here's the *real* question: How many decades must go by before the decade in question is considered a candidate for the oldies group? I'm going to go out on a limb and say three. That gives me a few more years before I have to start stashing Werther's caramels in the pocket of my tattered bathrobe and yelling at kids to get off my lawn.

I'm one of those people who allows a song to take me on a journey. I've been on this planet for a little more than forty years, and a handful of bands and musicians have permanent places in my heart because their music is the soundtrack of my life.

My love for music stemmed from my obsession with Broadway and evolved seamlessly through the ages. The first musical I ever experienced was *A Chorus Line*, live at the Strand Theater in Shreveport, Louisiana. We sat on the back row, and I could not have been happier. That theatrical affair was soon followed by *Cats*, *Phantom of the Opera*, and *Les Misérables*.

My first New York musical was *Wicked*. Solid choice, right? My first theater gasp was during *The Lion King* as I studied the cheetah gracefully crawl across the stage. My first rush to purchase the soundtrack was *Hamilton*.

And the first time I thought I was going to be banned from a major theater was with my mother. Ironically, we were seeing *Mamma Mia*.

I somehow scored front-row tickets to the show in New York City, right beside the conductor, who has a bit part at the end. Mama, who sat right next to the man, kept talking to him about how she liked the show and what a great job he was doing. The poor man nodded and smiled, all while keeping perfect time with his baton. When some of the actors got close to the edge of the stage and made eye contact with Mama, she reached out to touch them. True story. This happened twice.

Between that and her conductor accolades, I'm sure our names are on some blackball list, forbidding us from ever visiting West 44th Street until the end of time.

The '80s introduced me to boy bands, hair bands, and one-hit wonders. With the onset of grunge rock (no, thank you), I two-stepped my way through the '90s and added country music to my repertoire.

By the time I reached college, I had submerged myself into contemporary Christian. My eclectic collection was impressive, yet a heavy cloud lingered over my Panasonic stereo. While everyone else was buying generators and stocking up on cases of water for the doomsday known as Y2K, I agonized over which cassette tapes to replace with a CD format.

Here's something I do not love: purging music.

First and foremost, I acknowledged that this decision would be life-altering and that it was natural to suffer from acid reflux because of it. The second thing I did was kiss my dad's feet for helping me buy a car that had both a CD player and cassette tape deck.

Finally, I did the math. Logic dictates that all one-hit wonders or artists with only a few good songs on an album will be transitioned to a single mixtape of musical bliss. This brilliant accord alone culled my collection in half.

I decided a solid foundation could be built upon the following:

- *The Immaculate Collection*—Madonna
- *Urban Cowboy* Soundtrack
- *Greatest Hits*—Journey
- *Chicago—Greatest Hits: 1982–1989*
- *The Very Best of Prince*
- *Bad*—Michael Jackson
- *Slippery When Wet*—Bon Jovi
- *The Joshua Tree*—U2
- *When Harry Met Sally* Soundtrack
- *Ropin' the Wind*—Garth Brooks
- *Grease* Soundtrack
- *Jagged Little Pill*—Alanis Morissette
- *Let's Talk About Love*—Celine Dion
- *Life Love & Other Mysteries*—Point of Grace
- *Newsies* Soundtrack
- *Once Upon a Christmas*—Kenny Rogers and Dolly Parton
- Disney Classics Box Set
- *Monster Ballads*—Tagline: "Every bad boy still has his soft side."

As the years passed, my collection grew. My heartburn returned when digital tracks entered my world, but I survived by making playlists to help me cope with yet another media.

The artists in my box of old cassette tapes, CD cases, and iTunes have been supporting me my entire life. The fact that

I can visit my musical friends anytime I want makes me giddy. They get me through long road trips, housecleaning, manuscript writing, dance parties, and dinner dates. But nothing compares to live music. Unless you count the conjured gospel choir that often accompanies me in my car, I will always support listening to any artist in a natural habitat. The art of acquiring tickets for a popular concert nowadays haunts my dreams at night. Even if you're sitting at your computer, hitting refresh every few minutes, your best laid plans for securing decent venue seats can be thwarted if you're not paying attention. That's why I nominate other people to do it for me. Except for the time I wanted to go to a Garth Brooks concert.

Bulls, Blood, Dust, Mud

In 2015, my preferred country music radio station deejays announced that Garth Brooks would be coming to Houston on tour. Immediately my phone blew up. My friends were ecstatic. Our fearless leader, Emily, had been tracking (read: stalking) his website for months. And now our dreams were about to become a reality. We marked our calendars, waiting with anticipation for the hour we could purchase our tickets. Ten of us were committed to the cause, yet only two could commit to the actual purchase of said tickets.

Emily and me.

The pressure was tremendous. Tickets were sold in a raffle format. That meant every single seat in Toyota Center was a flat $75. Once you signed on and chose a day and time, the computer assigned you a seat based on a combination of random selection and your place in line. Emily and I also prayed it up for good measure. We wanted all our bases covered.

Ticket day finally rolled around, and Ticketmaster robots told us we needed to be ready to order at 10:00 a.m. sharp. Naturally, Emily called me two hours prior to make sure I was up and ready.

I was already hitting refresh.

Because Emily is a smart person, she'd read her instructional emails, which mentioned an important detail I'd skimmed right over. We had to start standing in a virtual line at 9:00 a.m. Around 8:45, Emily called to discuss timing, nervous stomachs, and the reality that we may have to sit in the nosebleed section if we weren't completely focused on the task at hand.

Suddenly Emily tells me her computer has changed. She's in virtual line! And it's only 8:54! I quickly refresh my screen. I'm in virtual line too! What does it all mean?

Who cares? I can finally go to the bathroom. Moments like these give me the runs.

Emily and I check in with each other only via text, forcing ourselves to do some actual work. But it's no use. Soon we're back on the phone, staring at our computers in silence. Ticketmaster tells us a small digital man will begin running across the bottom of our screens when the time comes. Emily reminds me to log in to my account to see if I remember my password and if my information is correct. Every second we can shave off may make a difference.

We wait. And wait. And wait some more. When the clock strikes 10:00 . . .

Lincee: "There he is! My man popped up! Do you see your man?"
Emily: "Yes! I have a man!"

Emily: "My man isn't really running."
Lincee: "Mine isn't either. It's more of a saunter."

Emily: "This is not a running man. This is a walking man."
Lincee: "My man is broken—"

In a split-second, my man began running across the bottom of my screen. I had no time to adjust. I just started screaming in Emily's ear—helpful things like "What do I do?" and "How many tickets am I buying?" and "What do I do!"

The screen changes. Ticketmaster asks me for the date I want. I choose, and only one time is provided. I take it. Emily shouts encouragements from the other end. I select my number of tickets and choose the versatile one-click button for my purchase convenience. I click a few boxes, agree to a few terms, and wait for the results.

Floor. Tenth row. Section A.

Lord, help me.

I keep my cool, because Emily is now screaming that her man is running. She goes through the same process I did, excited to announce that she's on the floor too!

We celebrate our stellar ticket purchasing skills through a mass email with the others. This concert is going to be epic. There's only one thing left to do: decide what to wear.

The day of the show, you'd find all ten of us standing in the blistering heat outside Toyota Center, waiting for the 7:00 p.m. audience to exit the building. It was 10:00. As in p.m. Not one of us complained about the fact that we couldn't get in until 10:30, for an 11:30 p.m. show.

How awesome was Garth Brooks for doing two shows in one night?

Some of us may have taken naps in prep for the evening's late festivities. We all wanted to prove we were still young and fabulous, like the kids nowadays who get ready to roll up into the club about this time.

Did kids still roll up into clubs? I didn't know. What I did know was the concert wouldn't start for another hour and a half. *Help me, Rhonda.* And since Toyota Center and Ticketmaster both told us to be at the venue no later than 9:00, we'd already had a lot of time to waste as we stood in the warm exhaust fumes of a parked bus. The main focus of our conversation revolved around which Garth Brooks song we were most looking forward to hearing. What I loved about the exchange was that no two answers were the same.

We finally got through the cattle call and into the actual building, where we took great pride in loudly asking, "Where do we go if we have *floor seats?*" It was fabulous. And so were the seats.

Garth Brooks was everything I hoped he would be. He sounded exactly like he had in my car so many years ago. He was passionate, energetic, and humble.

Also, everyone loved my T-shirt that read "Blame it all on my East Texas roots." Wearing the concert tee to the concert is a major fashion faux pas. But designing an original tee that flaunts one's love of the musical act is totally acceptable for a throwback concert.

You'll be labeled a dork if you do this at an indie or folk concert, however. Trust me. I know.

I was introduced to Mumford & Sons in 2009. The song "Roll Away Your Stone" was among their tracks, but I was a bit of a slow mover and didn't drink the Mumford Kool-Aid right away.

About a year later, I stopped in my tracks when I heard "Below My Feet" while preparing for a trip to Africa. This was the moment I decided to investigate the band. Through careful analysis, I fell in love with other songs on the *Sigh No More* and *Babel* albums, respectively. I fully drank the Mumford & Sons Kool-Aid with a large crazy straw and a stack of seasonal Oreos on the side. When the band announced they were coming to Houston on tour, I elected my friends Amy and Susan to go with me.

Thirty seconds into the gut-wrenching, blood pressure–spiking, butt-clenching ticket-buying process, Amy scored three tickets on the open lawn in the outdoor pavilion. We were among the fans who arrived at the venue when the doors opened two hours before the performance, so we could stake our claim front and center. It was worth it. From beginning to end, I was filled with joy, sorrow, angst, and then joy again. For the longest time, I tried to figure out what it was about these guys that made me so happy. The answer came to me at this concert. The members of Mumford & Sons are passionate about their music, their instruments, their lyrics, their fans, and their friendship. You can feel it in the air. It's contagious. And we were lucky enough to see it up close and personal.

Go get 'em, Marcus! Aggressively stomp that pedal drum and manically strum your guitar. That harmonica holder looks great on you!

Ah, harmonica holders. My sweet spot.

Susan said something that night that has stuck with me ever since we serenaded "Little Lion Man" back to the stage. She and Amy are both musicians, and they also love the theater. I pretend I'm half as educated as they are when the three of us are together. I mainly nod my head and file away what they say so I can Google it later.

Susan looked around at everyone in the venue. They were all holding up their phones, trying to capture red-letter moments.

Susan: "This is so sad."

Lincee: "What?"

Susan: "They're watching the show through tiny screens. They're missing it."

That's the beauty of live music. Absorb your surroundings. Listen for the slight differences in musical arrangement between recordings and what you're hearing. Watch the faces on stage. Raise your hands. Feel the rhythm. Try holding off finding the right song to show the world on InstaStories how you were halfway connected to a fabulous moment in time. Instead, fully connect to that fabulous moment in time.

Stop experiencing life through a tiny screen and just experience life. Let the weight of the talent seep into your subconscious. Allow the genius to take root so it's a part of your forever.

If I hear "Shake It Off" by Swifty, I think of my friend Autumn finagling us into the VIP section near the stage and how I tried to get Sarah to tattoo "Wildest Dreams" somewhere daring on her body. She didn't, but wouldn't that be a fun memory for that song?

Say Michael Bublé, and I remember Keri helping me up from a parking lot in Austin after I tripped over nothing in my chunky wedges on the way to the concert venue. When I hear "Freedom" by George Michael, I'm reminded of the inebriated groupie sitting next to me, who kept screaming for George to sing "Free Bird." Cool song, drunk girl. Wrong band.

At a Michael W. Smith concert, I hooked arms with a line of grown adults from my church and swayed to "Friends Are Friends Forever." It was not a satirical moment. I called Baton Rouge with an arena full of Garth Brooks–loving individuals. The Judds built a bridge between their hearts and mine, and I never looked back.

Live entertainment is powerful. Lyrics can act as a gentle tranquilizer to your soul, or they can wiggle their way into your head, attaching a specific song with a specific memory. We can crack up admitting we've misheard the words of beloved songs for years, sometimes for decades, and sit humbly as a melody pulled straight from someone's personal experience washes over us the exact moment we need to hear it.

Some songs energize and fill me with hope that my one true love is just around the corner. How deep is my love? Why, I'm not sure, Barry Gibb, but I'm willing to find out. Peter Cetera doesn't want to live without my love. Indeed, he does not. Have you ever sung a duet with Tim McGraw as if you were Faith Hill professing your love? Why not?

George Strait has told me many times that I look so good in love, and I appreciate the accurate observation. I agree with Janet Jackson that love will never do without you. I've experienced a groovy kind of love, an everlasting love, doing anything for love, a vision of love, and wings of love. A universal sentiment adopted by many and championed by the Beatles is that all you need is love.

Ironically, another universal sentiment adopted by many, and championed by Def Leppard, is that love bites.

16

You Give Love a Bad Name

For those of us who **LOVE** *a Burn Book*

I'm no stranger to heartache. In my first book, *Why I Hate Green Beans*, I spend a couple of chapters sharing the story of my high school sweetheart, who later became my husband. This is the part where some of you get excited about me launching into a glowing account of how my marriage was just like my beloved Emily Blunt and John Krasinski's, except I'm not a superstar, nor do I have a British accent.

You're too cute. That is nowhere near my story.

Once upon a time, my knight-in-shining-armor husband was unfaithful and decided to reboot his life with another woman. His indiscretion ripped my heart to shreds and caused my entire world to come crumbling down around me in a heap. I invite you to pick up a copy of my memoir, so you can read for yourself how I went from a blushing bride doting on her handsome husband to a crazed divorcée with an unnatural attachment to a pair of gray Buc-ee's sweatpants, Cheetos, and the TV show *Friends*. You'll laugh, you'll cry, and you'll bless my heart.

I've been single since the morning he left almost fourteen years ago. You'd think I would be used to him not being around, but the truth is I think about him often. Anytime I go home to Hallsville, I'm positive I see him driving his truck around town or pulling into the gas station. Burnt orange reminds me of his love for the Texas Longhorns. As I pull up the driveway to my parents' house, I see visions of our wedding day. I see the white tents, the gorgeous cake, the dance floor, and the catering wagons where Daddy is frying up catfish for the reception.

Rogue pictures of him pop up in boxes, photo albums, or drawers that haven't been opened in years. We had code words and inside jokes that still make me smile. Then I feel stupid for smiling. Why am I smiling at the guy who caused me to struggle with so much insecurity?

I was sure he was the one. Mrs. Lee all but told me he was. For real. She predicted that the guy in the white lab coat who loves fossils was named Nelson. He didn't have a lab coat, but do you know what my ex-husband's middle name is? Nelson.

I had everything planned out. I felt all the feelings. We did everything in the right order. I loved him with every fiber of my being. And it still didn't work out.

I can quickly go down a dark, dark path if I think about what my future looks like if I never find someone to share the remaining years of my life. I apologize for the depressing interlude, but it's a legitimate fear. I have become hyperaware of the fact that something feels missing from my heart.

I associate the overwhelming void I feel with someone's love for me. I don't feel complete. Time dictates that overwhelming void will be filled or it won't. That reality is equally hopeful and downright terrifying.

I haven't come close to rebuilding what I once had with my own Prince Charming. People tell me my time will come. These are the folks who remind me how many times the Bible instructs us to wait. They also tell me patience is a virtue.

I understand what they mean. I'm going to wait patiently right now as I try not to think about punching them in the sternum.

That is a contentious reaction, and I will justify my response as soon as you stop wondering why I'm not tackling the digital dating world, dropping my virtual hankie, or swiping right at all the potential suitors in my age range. May I point you to the entirety of part 5 in my first book? It explains everything. Online dating is weird and scary, and I'm happy to joyfully participate on the sidelines as a support system for my friends who dare enter its waters.

Who knows what I should do this far into the game? One part of me believes if I'm supposed to meet Mr. Right in the produce department, then eventually I'm going to one day decide to go to the grocery store, fall madly in love with the guy thumping cantaloupes, and that will be all she wrote.

Well, technically that won't be all she wrote. She'll probably write a third book about how she found love in an H-E-B supermarket one hot summer day by pretending to like cantaloupe so the gentleman who looks exactly like Latino pop star Ricky Martin would teach her how to tell if a melon is ripe. I shall title the memoir *Livin' La Vida Loca* and will set up all the necessary arrangements for Drew Barrymore to play me in the movie version.

Another part of me believes I should recruit several friends to see if they would like to enter into what I'm calling "The Golden Girls Agreement." I say if we're all over a certain age, we embrace the camaraderie of strong-willed Dorothy, spacey Rose, Southern belle Blanche, and crusty old Sophia and live together. Let's go all-in and move to Miami, sit at the kitchen table eating cheesecake, and talk about our nonexistent love lives and what it was like in the good ole days.

Dibs on Rose.

Speaking of roses, our culture seems to have divided the female gender into two distinct categories: the one who gets the rose and the one who doesn't. Of course, the one who got the rose is also in a third category, scarred by the thorns and forced to dramatically remove the bud from the stem in great frustration, only to have her mother offer to make a nice potpourri from the discarded crimson petals.

Nowhere are these categories more obvious than in our music. It crosses every genre. For every heart-and-soul mixtape that honors an assortment of country and western declarations, '90s R&B hits, and anything a crooner sings from the Great American Songbook is an anti-version of survival messages, girl-power anthems, and unnecessary declarations of future violence directed at a cheater's automobile.

Research proves that sad love songs are easier to write. Everyone has experienced a broken heart in one way or another, but most have trouble putting how they feel into words. Or they shove it down into the bottom sections of their hearts to be dealt with later. If a lyric manages to elicit an emotion that forces the listener to revisit the pain, the writer has done his or her job.

Sad love songs are often the soothing balm my heartache needs. Knowing someone else identifies with my suffering makes the world feel less lonely. I'm proficient in this space, and I have an entire playlist devoted to the genre.

The playlist is labeled "Onions," because listening to it will undoubtedly send me into a fit of tears.

Several songs stir up memories of lost love, like Wynona's belting of "Strongest Weakness." I allow myself to turn back the clock and quietly reflect when I push play. "In the Garden" was performed at Mimi's funeral, and when I hear Elvis Presley sing it, I give myself permission to cry because I miss her terribly. "Adonai" by Avalon got me through my divorce. The All Sons & Daughters' live version of "Great Are You Lord" helped me through a time when I wanted to sit in darkness for just a little too long.

None of us are immune to heartache. Whether a broken heart is the result of a death, a breakup, a rejection, or an unrequited longing, music seems to strum the stings of that broken heart like no other medium.

Consider King David in the Bible. Much of the book of Psalms is a journal of heart cries David wrote, often to be set to music. Perhaps that's why people gravitate toward his psalms. Within the vast array of emotions he expressed, almost everyone finds a familiar cry, ache, fear, or praise.

King David was the king of mixtapes.

Within that scriptural mixtape I have found a balm for my soul. A ballad for my singleness. When I feel adrift, unchosen, without a rose or a fairy-tale ending, I'm reminded of a deeper truth: God is my portion forever. Although my flesh and heart may fail, He is my strength. Psalm 73 gives me the assurance that I am enough. He chose me. He loves me. The God who spoke the universe into existence chose me even with my freak-ishly spelled name. He chose me understanding that I can eat Skittles only by color. I hear the lyrics of love in this psalm of acceptance, and my heart beats to the rhythm of being in sync with someone who totally gets me.

And He says I'm worthy of much more than a rose.

17

Love Is a Battlefield

For those of us who didn't know we
were on a break from **LOVE**

Look, I accept the fact that love stories aren't for everyone. It's a tough world out there, and you might be in a place where you'd just as soon spit in the face of love if it dared to come near you during this vulnerable time. I get it.

Or you simply might not buy into this squishy love stuff. I *don't* get that. Nevertheless, I'm here for you.

I'd like to address all the readers out there who have no use for my love story enlightenment. You're the ones who choose to embrace a more cerebral and, dare I say, complex version of romance. You are *The Handmaid's Tale* to my *Gilmore Girls*. The "I don't have time to go to the movies" to my movie theater club card. The NPR podcast to my *The Greatest Showman* soundtrack.

This chapter is a belly-flop look into some ridiculous break-ups. I know you skeptics reading this are excited for the lack of grating lovey-dovey talk, but let me point out that most of these miserable moments were immediately followed by the brokenhearted taking to her bed, staring at her poster of stunning Jordan Catalano, confident he would never kiss another girl once they were going together. The bedroom is filled with the discord of Sinéad O'Connor's "Nothing Compares to You" on repeat as a healthy binge of romantic classics (see *Sleepless in Seattle, Hitch, The Proposal,* and *Win a Date with Tad Hamilton!*) play on a loop, which don't stand a chance of drowning out hormonal tears of rage.

Or something like that.

Remember when Berger broke up with Carrie on a Post-it note in *Sex and the City*? The crushing blow read, "I'm sorry. I can't. Don't hate me." This is the kind of madness we're talking about. I've collected a sampling of equally horrendous breakup stories from dear friends and loyal readers who were kind enough to share these memories—as long as I changed the names to protect the half-wits.

Prepare for your love palate to be cleansed, you nonbelievers.

Laura—FRIENDSWOOD, TEXAS

In seventh grade I got a bad perm. The first red flag: I got it at Montgomery Ward. It's the Walmart to the Target that is JCPenny. The second red flag: my hairdresser was channeling Billy Idol with his own haircut. To say I looked like a poodle when it was over is offensive to poodles everywhere. My bangs were fried for a year. My boyfriend broke up with me because, he said, "Even though I like her, I just wish she'd brush her hair."

Donna—ATLANTA, GEORGIA

A guy I broke up with handed my sister an envelope. Inside was an invoice in the amount of $423.60 for all the dates he had paid for over the course of the five weeks we dated. He not only charged me for the meals and movie tickets he had purchased but also decided to toss in "wear and tear" on his car, which included an oil change. Thankfully he credited me for a pot-roast lunch I had made for him one Sunday after church.

Kirsten—HOUSTON, TEXAS

I dated a British guy when I was studying abroad. I learned he was irritatingly emotional and very demanding when we took a trip to Ireland. I finally could not take it anymore, so I dumped him in Dublin. He immediately began bawling and yelling and making a huge scene. Irish people all watched the British guy and the American girl who broke his heart in the middle of the street. Like an animal.

Holly—TULSA, OKLAHOMA

When I was fourteen, I broke up with my first boyfriend by telling him, "I never really liked you that much. I just thought you were cute." I couldn't understand why he thought that was so rude. I told him he was cute!

Paula—HOUSTON, TEXAS

We spent the afternoon at the Museum of Fine Art. That night we had dinner at his parents' house. I'd been there many times before, but suddenly I realized the art he loved was his mom's paint by number paintings.

They were everywhere in the house, and I knew they would positively be in his own house someday. But not mine. I dumped him the next day. No regrets.

Sherilyn—SURREY, BRITISH COLUMBIA, CANADA

I found out my high school boyfriend had broken up with me when I learned he had transferred to another school.

Jennifer—BRISTOW, VIRGINIA

My friends agreed to break up with my boyfriend for me while we were hanging out at the mall. (The mall was this place kids went to walk around and eat Chick-fil-A before they made their drive-through operations so efficient.) My friends called him for me on a pay phone. (This was a phone attached to a wall that you had to put a whole quarter in to use.) He wasn't home, so they left a message for him on the family's answering machine. (It's kind of like a voice mail, but on an itty-bitty cassette tape shared by the whole family.) "Hey, Guy!" the spokesperson said. "I'm just calling to let you know that our friend doesn't want to go out with you anymore. Have a great night."

Brooke—ATLANTA, GEORGIA

Things had been off for a while. We sat down on his couch, and I straight-up asked if he thought we should still be together. He said nothing. Zero, zip, nada. I stood up and walked out, and we never spoke again. I guess by technical standards we might still be together.

Susie—PUEBLO, COLORADO

A guy I was dating broke up with me via text. While I was home sick. On Valentine's Day.

Jessica—FAIRFAX, VIRGINIA

My high school boyfriend broke up with me on my birthday—in my yearbook.

Grace—HOUSTON, TEXAS

An hour before my heart surgery, my boyfriend waltzed into my hospital room to tell me he hadn't been happy in months. Forty minutes later, after I tried to bargain with him about getting counseling and that we can change, blah, blah, blah, I looked down at my already prepped chest beneath my hospital gown. I was having my heart broken twenty minutes before I was wheeled back to fix my actual broken heart. I relented: "Okay, well I can't stop you from wanting to break up. You can leave now." On his way out he accidentally knocked over my yellow Gatorade. I really needed those electrolytes.

Christa—COLUMBUS, OHIO

My boyfriend surprised me one morning while I was working from home. He showed up at my door with breakfast. Then he broke up with me. Nothing says "Have a nice life" like a basket full of blueberry mini muffins.

Katie—HOUSTON, TEXAS

I once dated and broke up with an entire band. Not on purpose and not all at once. Throughout high school and college, I dated the guitar player, the bassist, and the drummer on separate occasions. They should have named their band Katie's Exes.

Alyce—LANCASTER, PENNSYLVANIA

I broke up with a guy, and a few months later he sent me an email explaining a talk he was going to give at church. A talk wherein I was blamed for his "quarter-life crisis." I couldn't find a direct link to the good news of the gospel of Jesus Christ. Instead, he quoted *Star Trek 2: The Wrath of Khan* a lot.

Rinn—BEDFORD, TEXAS

A guy I was dating gave me an ultimatum: Give up Dr Pepper and sugar F-O-R-E-V-E-R or our relationship was over. I chose sugar. He didn't understand how I could love food more than him. I couldn't understand why he was so crazy.

Leah—HOUSTON, TEXAS

I got dumped before a blind date. He told me he forgot he was already dating someone.

Kelli—DENVER, COLORADO

After two years of dating, my boyfriend announced that we were just not compatible because I didn't understand his feelings. I was insensitive because I had thrown away one of his love notes, which read, "Have a really good day at work. Love you!"

maggie—LINCOLN, NEBRASKA

I had been saving up for a down payment on a house. When I told my boyfriend, he said, "Women don't buy houses. Men buy houses that women live in." That's when I decided I was definitely buying a house and definitely breaking up with him. I adopted a dog and never looked back.

Paige—BIRMINGHAM, ALABAMA

My fiancé broke off our engagement over text message while I was at home dealing with my aunt's death.

Renni—ASHBURN, VIRGINIA

My boyfriend of three years was the manager of a local restaurant. I found out he was unfaithful from a review on Yelp. "The sour beer is pretty good, courtesy of the cheating manager."

mandie—DALLAS, TEXAS

A guy broke up with me after five dates because I hadn't noticed he had a prosthetic arm. It's okay, because earlier that day he asked me to shave his back. Hard pass.

What doesn't kill you makes you stronger, right? That's what Kelly Clarkson says. I say what doesn't kill you makes you question every decision you've ever made about your future with a guy who didn't even know you were crushing on him. Kelly should write a song about that.

18

Feel the Burn

*For those of us who would **LOVE** to be
in the Fitness Protection Program*

Heartache often shares territory with the love story in one form or another. Enduring the heaviness is part of life. When you experience it, I propose you hole up in a sunless room with Mark Darcy, Adele's greatest hits, and a tube of chocolate chip cookie dough. That should get you through the first few hours.

I like that these items are simple and uncomplicated, and that I have a system in place that's been proven successful in soothing one's suffering.

What I don't have is a way to tackle the dreaded love/hate relationship. This is the awkward third cousin once removed from heartache. These are tricky waters one must navigate carefully. You know you're supposed to love, or even just like the situation, yet everything inside you wants to run in the other direction.

This kind of relationship might be with your great-aunt Tilley. She's always in your business in a passive-aggressive way, and she won't stop hounding you about coming to visit her more often in the remote Oklahoma town where she lives. Her discovery of Facebook made for a bleak day. Sure, you can hide her from your social media feed, but the fact remains that Tilley will always be a prominent branch on your family tree. She's "ride or die," and you will be speaking at her funeral one day.

Another example is your relationship with Netflix. Has there ever been an invention as life-changing as this one? I think not. An entire world of entertainment can be accessed with the click of one button. If bingeing is wrong, you don't want to be right. You applaud your time management skills as you calculate all the hours you're saving by not watching commercials. Then something vexing happens. Netflix pops up a little screen, prompting you to confess you really are still watching even though it's been three hours since you logged on.

Stop cramping my style, Netflix. I'm going through some things right now, and your delightful original programming is the only thing that can get me through it. Back off!

Or you may have both loving and hateful feelings toward something as innocent as a creamy bowl of queso. It's never steered you wrong. Even so, you understand that consuming too much of its rich goodness is unwise. Trying to convince yourself that you'll dip only five chips proves to be a futile endeavor and will unavoidably result in you sobbing as you stand on the bathroom scale later in the week.

As for me, I've been sparring with the same love/hate relationship for years. Allow me to introduce you to my number one frenemy: exercise.

Swimming

Young Lincee was an active child. I rode my pink bike over the river and through the woods to my friend Linna's house every day for an entire summer. I was also a superior roller-skater.

Since we didn't have a roller-skating rink in our town, Mama let us skate on the concrete around the swimming pool to the *Grease* soundtrack.

That's right. We hand jived on eight wheels around a deep body of water in six-pound shoes that could sink us to the bottom in a matter of nanoseconds. We also skated on the trampoline.

Mother was present during all these shenanigans. I'm sure she was right there, desperately trying to finish out the roll on her Kodak Disc camera as we zipped by, before running downtown to Mike's. The local pharmacist was also our photo developer. I guarantee that wheel of film consisted of nothing but flowers and landscaping. Who needs precious memories of the children you carried in your womb for nine months when your Christmas cactus is blooming? That's the moment you should preserve for all prosperity.

Jamie and I once asked Mama why she let us roller-skate around the pool when she knew that if we fell in, we would plummet to the bottom. Without hesitation, she replied, "Oh, I thought about that a lot. That's why we bought y'all Velcro skates. And remember how your Daddy would grab you and force you underwater for several minutes when he was teaching you how to swim? We knew you needed to practice holding your breath. If you fell in, you would calmly whip off your skates and swim to the top. And then probably dive back down to retrieve your skates at the bottom. We never worried about you girls. You were always strong swimmers."

Safety first. That's our family motto.

Growing up around a pool was wonderful. I was the blonde kid whose hair turned green thanks to my never-ending efforts to nail my synchronized swimming routine.

I mastered most tricks on the diving board. The one I was most proud of was my backflip. I executed it in pike position, and I'm certain it would have won me a gold medal in the Sydney Summer Olympics if I hadn't been so self-conscious about my green hair. My art suffered as a result. I could have been great.

As the years passed, I realized swimming involved me wearing a bathing suit in front of people. I took a hiatus from my pseudo exercise routine for a decade, choosing instead to walk a mile in my neighborhood. I opted for watching Hulu during the months when outside felt like the surface of the sun.

The year rash guards became a thing was the best year of my life. Swimming in a long-sleeved shirt and shorts? *Hallelujah! Summer Olympics, here I come!*

On the Fourth of July, I was frolicking in my parents' pool with eight children and three adults. Being the cool grownup I am, I was the only grownup participating in "Diving Board Games," as they're called at the Ray household. Basically, those in the pool challenge the daredevil kids (and one full-grown woman) to answer a question mid-jump.

I had just correctly answered "eight" after my brother-in-law called out the square root of sixty-four (we like to educate as well as play) when I popped up by my sister in the shallow end. She said she was proud of me!

Wait, proud that I was able to both recall and blurt out the answer in such a small sliver of time while in midair? Or proud that I knew the answer? I stood there, contemplating if I should be offended. To test the water (pun intended) I casually wondered out loud if I should do a backflip off the diving board.

Jamie: "I don't think so."
Lincee: "You don't think I should? Or you don't think I can?"
Jamie: [silence]

Challenge accepted, dear sister.

I marched my happy self up to the diving board to the chortles of my entire family. Half were rooting for me because they wanted to point and laugh when I ended up doing a belly flop.

The other half were scared I'd crack my head open. I remember Mama screaming, "Don't do this! You're not a young girl anymore!"

Game on, Mother.

I whipped out yet another beautiful backflip in pike position. I'd appreciate it if you never tell any of the witnesses that my entire right side hurt for a week.

Dancing

Swimming, skating, and riding my bike never felt like exercise. I was just a kid baking in the sun, scraping my knee, and coasting down a hill. Activity was a fact of life.

The love/hate rapport with exercise hit full-on loathing in junior high.

One day my physical education teacher made me jog a mile around the school property. That was the day I decided running is for people who need to have their heads examined. Cross-country felt like a sick joke. One should sprint only when being chased by a murderer or vicious animal.

Who are you marathon people, and why would you ever do that to your body? I don't care if the medals are in the shape of the Millennium Falcon. *Calm down and keep your running group away from me. I don't want to catch your fever, you weirdos.*

Where was I?

Oh yes. I make a list of goals on the first day of January every year. One of those recurring bullet points is the mandate to "lose twenty pounds." I'm nothing if not consistent.

Will you find me doing BODYPUMP at the YMCA after work or on a brisk six-mile run before dinner? No. Do I enjoy the euphoria that accompanies most physical activity? Of course I do. I've watched Elle Woods in *Legally Blonde* enough times to know that exercise gives you endorphins, and endorphins make you happy, and happy people don't shoot their husbands.

Where's the compromise? How can I walk that fine line between wanting to shoot someone and having the mental capacity to want to do the work?

I have a foolproof plan. I take it back to the basics. The way I trick my brain into tolerating exercise is by making it think we're just dancing.

Take salsa, for instance. I took a class at Life Time Fitness every Monday night for years, and I absolutely loved it. No, it didn't have anything to do with the *muy guapo* Roberto who taught the session.

Okay, it halfway had to do with *muy guapo* Roberto who taught the session. The first time I attended his class, I was asked to "please stand at the back of the room" by a gaggle of ladies way too old to be mean girls. I didn't understand. Did we have assigned spots on the floor? Was there a hierarchy of salsa aficionados?

Nope. It was just a bunch of older women who wanted to personally experience Roberto's pheromones. I get it. My face turned red when he and I made eye contact this one time and I incontrovertibly swallowed my tongue and choked. No one needs to see or hear that again.

I still curse the day when my schedule became compromised and I had to say *adios* to Roberto and his rhythmic hip gyrations. Oh, and I had to say good-bye to Life Time Fitness, too, which placed me in a precarious position. Where should I get my endorphins to keep me from murdering skinny women in Spandex?

Since I wasn't a cute twenty-three-year-old Rice University grad weighing twelve pounds, I didn't feel comfortable at my local 24 Hour Fitness. As if by divine intervention, I received a brochure in the mail about Jazzercise! Jazzercise is a dance class that throws in some aerobics for good measure. The class was in a community center less than a mile from my house. That meant if I was a runner, I could walk there.

Oh, don't think I didn't call that very day to inquire about Jazzercise. The lady I talked to was so nice. She enrolled me over the phone. Then she asked, "Are you available tonight?" I told her I was going to see the Harlem Globetrotters (stop laughing). Then she said, "Guess I'll see you bright and early in the morning, then!"

Six in the morning, to be exact.

I'm not afraid of the morning. I'm a happy morning person. However, six rolled around in the blink of an eye. Still, I was determined to start my day with a hearty helping of happy endorphins.

The best part of Jazzercising before the crack of dawn and living close to where you'll do it is that you can literally roll out of bed, go to the bathroom, brush your teeth, throw on a T-shirt and shorts, slip into some tennis shoes, pick a hat, and walk out the door.

That first morning I enter the community center and spy a perky young thing named Stacy in a lacy sports bra. Immediately I realize this is not the exercise I remember from my days of yore.

The Year Was 1982

The Ray household didn't have cable TV. Thankfully, the Clark household did. My friend Carmen recorded Mousercise on the Disney Channel for several weeks and loaned me the VHS tape. My sister, Jamie, and I followed the instructions from a darling woman and quickly learned that tying a grosgrain ribbon around the waist of our cotton leotards made them awesome to the max. Being in a dance family, we had a million leotards from which to choose. Also leg warmers. Oh, the leg warmers. Pick your color. We had it. Is it too hard because you're overwhelmed by the selection? Here. Wear my rainbow pair. I'm that cool.

The Year Was 1984

Jamie and I were introduced to Jane Fonda. We'd pop her cassette tape into my sister's Jambox and listen for Jane's instructions. I can still hear her asking us to grapevine to the left while Michael Jackson sang "Wanna Be Startin' Something." Our workout attire had advanced as well. We looked legit in our bright aquamarine unitards with complementary hot-pink briefs. *Only three more sets of ten, ladies!*

This present-day class was an interesting mixture of the old and the new. I was somewhere between. Stacy looked trendy in her lace top and Pilates pants. Nary a leg warmer was in sight. I was so glad I decided against my black parachute pants and "I Heart DANCE" off-the-shoulder number, selecting instead my New York Fire Department T-shirt and purple Nike shorts. Everyone over the age of fifty wore items made of Lycra, and two were sporting headbands.

Stacy bounded over to me, introduced herself, and asked if I was familiar with Jazzercise.

"Oh yes," I said. "I did Mousercise and Jazzercise in the '80s. I had no idea it was making a comeback."

Words cannot express the jerk of the head, squint of the eye, and power of Stacy's response: "Jazzercise never went anywhere. It's been around for decades."

Easy, Stacy. Let's loosen that microphone pack you have around your waist, okay, dear? Long live Jane Fonda. You go crank up "It's Raining Men" and we'll follow along.

To my surprise, we didn't Jazzercise to the Weather Girls. And Michael's *Off the Wall* album wasn't among Stacy's playlist. Heck no. Jazzercise has been around forever, and as a result the tunes have matured with the times.

Stacy had us bringing "Sexy Back" with JT as we marched across the floor. We bounced forever to Rhianna's "Shut Up and Drive." When Seal belted out "Amazing," my arms started shaking as I held up my little three-pound weights. I thought I was going to die.

I've never jumped so much in my life.

All and all, though, Jazzercise wasn't the key factor in my not losing twenty pounds that year. It probably had more to do with me stopping by Einstein Bagels every morning to reward myself for getting up so early and not passing out in class.

It's good to have goals.

19

You've Got a Friend in Me

For those of us who LOVE a BeFri necklace

My favorite movie about the love for a friend is *Beaches*. Miles, that hunk at my first high school dance, may be forever associated with the soundtrack, but the story is all mine. I'm a perpetual crier, so you can appreciate the sheer torture that runs through my brain when I flip through the TV channels and discover *Beaches* is on. This happens a lot more often than one would assume, because the 1988 classic is always on.

It's on Oxygen right now. I can feel it.

I will sit in anticipation, waiting for it to wreak havoc on my nervous system, even if it's way past my bedtime. Oh, only ten minutes of it are left? I'll watch.

I'll also cry.

The waterworks really kick in when Hillary convinces CC to take her to the beach house, knowing the end is near. She's not going to get a new heart. While playing a game of cards, CC casually mentions, "I know everything there is to know about you and my memory is long. Very, very long." CC bounces away into the house, and a fragile Hillary quietly responds, "I'm counting on it."

Tears. Jerking.

And although it's not my favorite, the "Wind Beneath My Wings" montage is a chance to really sob, with hard tears, cleansing your psyche from all its impurities.

The last minutes of the movie showcase CC singing "Glory of Love" as Hillary's daughter, Victoria, looks on from backstage. Then CC takes her hand and begins telling the story of how she first met Hillary when she was smoking under the Atlantic City boardwalk. The scene cuts to young Hillary and CC goofing around in a photo booth, with a lovely and equally haunting sound bite.

Hillary: "Be sure to keep in touch, CC, okay?"
CC: "Well sure. We're friends, aren't we?"

You may have met your own Hillary when you were a small girl in hot-pink fringe scampering around Atlantic City. You may have met your CC at a college party when no one else seemed to notice you were there. But however we've met her, this dear friend plays a significant role in our lives. We cherish her friendship. We crack a little at her brutal honesty. She knows what we need, when we need it. And we thank the Lord for the day she walked into our lives, because when the going gets tough, we can count on her faith, wisdom, strength, compassion, and ability to make comfort food without calories.

As corny as it may sound, you completely understand what it means to have this beloved friend as the wind beneath your wings. If you're not sitting next to her right now, go give her a call and tell her. Just phrase it differently, because she'll probably make fun of you for being an emotional wreck.

I have two friends I would call. I *have* called them, and neither one cares about Hillary or CC. But they do think I'm fabulous, so they indulge me on occasion. Rebecca and Jill have been with me since college, and we make a pretty spectacular team, if I do say so myself.

We're like a well-balanced scale. Rebecca is the left side, providing wise, logical advice with a no-nonsense attitude. I'm the right side, contributing emotional, empathetic, often tear-stained support between hiccups. Jill is the fulcrum, offering practical feedback with a sensitive touch.

For a long stretch of time I chose to stay with my husband even after learning of his infidelity. I didn't tell a soul what he'd done. I couldn't imagine this horrible dark cloud hanging over us at family gatherings or while we entertained friends around our dinner table. I believed we would work through this crippling time in our marriage, and I didn't want the past to dictate our future.

I kept it a secret. From my parents. From my sister. And from every single friend.

I quickly learned how to fake a normal life. I left chipper voice mail messages on phones. I blamed a busy schedule on work and a budding career. I conveniently had other plans anytime friends invited me to hang out.

But each day, I felt as though my husband was slipping more and more away from me, and as the months passed, I vowed to avoid anyone important to me until I had everything under control.

That's when Jill showed up unannounced. She knew her introverted friend wasn't living it up in the big city almost every night. My voice mails showcased an octave a little too squeaky in her opinion, and she sensed that even though my words were happy, my soul was not. She instinctively recognized that something was wrong, so she got in her car and drove five hours to get to the bottom of my weirdo behavior face-to-face.

When I opened the door, I steeled my bones to be strong. I willed my tear ducts to remain dry. I told myself I could easily pretend my life wasn't crumbling all around me.

That lasted thirty seconds.

Jill listened as I poured out my heart. She cried with me and never once said *this too shall pass* because she knew I would punch her in the trachea if she did. Like a good friend, she pumped me full of chips and queso and lightly chastised me for not including her during this pivotal time in my life. Then she gathered me into her arms to pray a desperate prayer to the Lord to spare me of this pain.

Last, she channeled her inner Rebecca and effortlessly put together a modified plan for my new future.

It was a significant moment in our friendship.

Sadly, I did get a divorce, but Jill and Rebecca were there every step of the way. We often escaped to my parents' house with all eight of their collective kiddos, so we could have alone time together. With all that land, the children ran wild as we sat on the back porch outlining my next steps.

Once, Rebecca and I were sitting in folding chairs out on the lawn while her son, Jack, intently watched as Daddy prepared a catfish for frying. My dad took him through each step, patiently explaining how to properly cut the perfect filet.

I couldn't help but imagine Jack as my own son, learning a skill from his grandfather. I'd always wanted to be a mom, and this was exactly how I'd imagined my life. Only that hope had just disappeared into oblivion.

I didn't say anything or make a sound as I watched Jack. I'm confident my posture didn't change. Not one tear escaped to drip down my cheek. I was a master of calm, cool, and collected even though my insides were breaking all over again.

It's as if we shared a brain. Rebecca's arm came around my shoulders, telling me she understood what I was feeling in that moment. Without saying a word, she was minding the gap, and with a single touch she let me know she would always be there for me.

We locked eyes, and I allowed one tear to drop. And then five. Followed by seventeen. Even though Rebecca isn't an affectionate person, she gently scratched my back as I felt all the sadness of what might have been.

I'm experienced at being the emotionally wrecked friend. I live there most days. When I was in junior high, one of my biggest worries was the coveted BeFri necklace. It was a heart broken in half with "BeFri" on one of the charms and "StEnd" on the other. Put them together and you've got best friends. Forgetting that society deemed the "StEnd" half of the charm less desirable, I had bigger problems to worry about. I was the recipient of two charms and the giver of zero, which stressed me out to no end.

I'm lucky. Today I would need an entire bucket of charms for all my people. Several dozen friends showed up for me this past year when I needed them the most. They supported me and celebrated my first book being launched into the world. They took over and demanded we rejoice that my lifelong dream had been fulfilled. They wanted to praise the reality that an actual book with my name on it existed, and that anyone could see it on a shelf at Barnes & Noble or in a shopping cart on Amazon.

They'll never know what it meant to me to walk into such a gorgeous venue, with divine decorations, elaborate food, thoughtful touches, and encouraging smiles and prayers the day of my launch. There's no way I can tell them. I can't do it. The thought leaves me weepy.

One nice young girl at the party asked me how many people in the room were related to me. I told her "just one" and pointed to Mama. She said, "So the rest are strangers and friends?" I answered yes. She looked at me, smiled, and said, "It must be nice to be surrounded by so much love. What a great community."

She's right.

Thirteen years ago, I drove into Houston with no idea what my future held. I was majorly depressed and a mirage of myself. Each one of my friends walked into my life, and in one way or another, they saved me from darkness.

Each one of them.

God knew waves of people in this big city would be ready to mind the gap. And He knew these individuals who pulled me from the hole I was in would be the exact same ones to celebrate my book when I was a nervous wreck.

February 2018 will go down in my own personal history as the day I allowed dear, sweet, loving friends to show up for me.

20

Birds of a Feather

For those of us who **LOVE** *the circle of life*

This is a difficult love/hate topic to write about, because I have such an amazing community of women and men who would do anything for me. That's the love part. My bench is deep, and I cherish each one.

The hate part of this equation is that I have a challenging time putting into words what these people mean to me. I'm disappointed in myself because I'll never be able to repay them for how they've enriched my life.

Also, I never wear my emotions on my sleeve.

Wait, let me rephrase that last sentence for those of you who know me well and are laughing hysterically. I never wear my emotions on *just* my sleeve. I take a bath in my feelings and walk around flinging them at anyone who will listen. This can be exhausting, but it's something with which I've learned to live.

Since words fail me, I find myself trying to show love through actions. It must be working, because my friend Catha gave me the kindest compliment at my fortieth birthday party. When asked to describe me, Catha answered, "Lincee shows up."

I was so proud in that moment. I adopted the praise and grafted it into my identity. If you need me, I will show up.

A few years ago, I had the opportunity to live out my slogan in riskier conditions, thanks to a now infamous case we like to call "The Circle of Life 2017."

I moved in with Lara the summer of 2016. We had been friends for years, but you don't truly know the ins and outs of someone's personality until you live with that someone.

For example, I may share that I like to take baths, making you think *Cool!* but then you continue reading Reese Witherspoon's book club list. If you lived with me, though, you'd quickly discover I take baths more than I take showers. The bathtub is a sanctuary for me. Bubbles are my life. I chose my very first apartment in Houston for its garden tub. True story.

Another example of my habits is that I eat like a kid. You probably imagine Chick-fil-A nuggets (yes) and maybe some mac and cheese (again, yes), but what you don't know is that I can happily live off Pringles, Belvita crackers, some sort of cheese, and fig Newtons for days. I would drink out of juice boxes and suck applesauce out of those pouches if it didn't get so many freakish looks from concerned adults and judgmental children.

Lara is no different. Well, she's a shower person with a healthy appreciation for all foods, but that's not the point. I was aware that she doesn't like birds. It wasn't until I lived with her that I realized the decryption for "doesn't like" is "Lord Jesus, save me!"

Thinking back to our woodpecker Woody and his dive-bombing tactics, I empathize with her terror. Lara would have never braved the attic to help Mama that day. She would have wanted to call Uber and escape to Sonic to wait for the all clear. And when she discovered that Hallsville doesn't have Uber, she would have started the five-mile trudge to downtown.

Woody was an extenuating circumstance. Your average bird doesn't have a daily plan to peck out your eyes. Lara realizes this and has developed a plan to simply avoid birds the best she can. With that said, land birds prove to be the hardest to dodge. Ducks are everywhere. I never notice them until I see my roommate tense in their presence.

When Lara and I were in Africa, we visited the Cheshire Homes orphanage. The lady in charge took us around the back of a building to see their new vegetable garden. I rounded the corner and was greeted by a thousand chickens. I turned to Lara behind me and gave her a look. No words were spoken, but she knew she needed to about-face and search for high ground.

A similar event unfolded closer to home later that year.

Lara and I commiserated by the glass back door of the house, watching a dove swoop up under the back porch over and over. Lara had been spying on it for days, and she was convinced the bird was making a nest somewhere near the house.

Lara enjoys the back porch, so this simply would not do. Mama had prepared me for this exact moment. I didn't have a swimming pool pole, but I did have a broom. I waved it around, shooing the dove away. Crisis averted.

The next morning, I found Lara poised at the back door again. She reported that she thought the bird had really built a nest this time, because in her opinion, the back-and-forth action she'd seen was way too much to think otherwise. I investigated, and sure enough, a collection of straw was on the porch table, right by the wall of the house.

I took the broom, swept the straw onto the ground, told the bird to find another back porch to crap on, and went inside.

I swept straw from the table six different times that day. This dove was not the leader of her fowl pack, if you catch my drift.

The following morning I checked the back porch and was shocked to see the dove had been busy building a legitimate, husky nest. She'd constructed her dwelling on top of the outdoor television. The TV was the floor of the nest, and the back of the house provided a nice barrier against predators and weather elements. The walls of the nest were constructed with various twigs, straw, leaves, and no telling what else, which I later learned were probably gathered for her by her man. I take it back. This dove was the valedictorian of her class with a PhD in nest building.

I hid this growing problem from Lara until she caught me sweeping the nest down on the ground and then resolved that being outside was overrated.

The next morning, we found a new nest mightier than its predecessor. Only this time, an egg was in there.

I reported my findings to Lara and patiently waited as she processed through all the feelings. Her emotions ranged from denial to *What fresh hell is this?* to bargaining. We surmised that the dove needed to go, the nest needed to go, and the TV needed to be saved from inevitable bird droppings leaking into its electrical circuits. Also, Lara needed to stop hyperventilating.

We both called parents for some sage advice about what to do with the nest with the egg.

My dad said, "Just knock it down" and then hung up on me. Lara's parents, Steve and Linda, suggested we pick it up and move it. There was just one problem with that plan. Mrs. Dove manufactured a nest without a bottom or one of its sides. We were looking at twigs in the shape of the letter C. With one egg daintily resting in the corner. Steve and Linda also suggested we call a guy friend to help us out.

The only guy we knew who could handle this delicate predicament was Todd, and he had just taken a dead possum from our friend Shanna's yard the week before. Todd deserved a pass on the "come get this critter" emergency phone tree.

I figured Jeremy couldn't step in again to help me puzzle through another animal crisis. I know a silly egg is way different from a dead cow, but Jeremy lives five hours away and probably wouldn't consider the request worthy of his time. Also, I have neither seen nor spoken to Jeremy in twenty years.

Lara reached the point of panic when she learned that removing a bird's nest is delicate work and costs the same as a car payment to have someone come and do it. I looked at my friend and then made a decision.

I grabbed a brown bag with a cute handle from Magpies gift shop. I put on a rubber glove and hauled the stepladder outside. I summoned all the courage of my mother and crawled up to face the nest head-on. Then I swept the entire thing, including the little egg, into the bag and ran it to the trash can.

The guilt I felt for my contribution to the circle of life was assuaged when I walked back into the house to find Lara with the confidence to experience fresh air again. Her fear had been replaced with celebratory champagne.

The day I showed up for Lara is a day that will live in infamy. It's also the day people called me an animal hater, but that's okay. Lara's emotional well-being will always come before a bird, every time.

21

Addie Lou Who

For those of us who LOVE our "Best Aunt Ever" T-shirts

I have always been a great fisherwoman. Why, I was a mere six years old when I caught my first perch all by myself. I begged Daddy to let me cast and reel on my own. He was happy for me to embrace my independence, but extremely irritated that I had little to no patience when it came to waiting for my bobber to go under when a fish finally bit my worm. Frustrated, he left me at the edge of the pond and climbed back on his tractor, making plans to set something on fire later.

I remember casting. I remember reeling. And I remember singing "The sun will come out, tomorrow" with the gusto of someone who loved a red-headed orphan. I felt a tug, so I reeled some more, and out popped what other fish in that pond probably called "dinner."

I didn't care that I had used bait to catch bigger bait. I started jumping up and down, trying to get Daddy's attention. He finally saw me with a fish in my hand and ran over to congratulate his beaming daughter. We made the trek up to the house. Mama snapped several shots of me holding my prize-winning fish in dramatic poses by her freshly potted bougainvillea. She was killing two birds with one stone on this roll of film.

I distinctly remember my haircut was Dorothy Hamill–inspired, my pink socks were pulled up to my knees, and either Strawberry Shortcake or Rainbow Brite was on my T-shirt. I high-fived everyone, asked if I could keep the fish, got upset when my mother wasn't convinced that yes, it could live in the swimming pool, and begrudgingly handed my catch to my father, who released it back into the wild to grow big and strong.

Between the thirty-minute photo shoot ordeal and my squeezing the little booger in a death grip, odds are that tiny perch never made it. Sad for him. Good memories for me.

Fast-forward several decades to a similar bright sunny day down by the pond. The Dorothy Hamill haircut had thankfully been replaced by a tussled beach wave trend with fantastic highlights. Even though I still wore a fun graphic tee, I embraced being older and perfectly capable of catching my own fish without my father's help.

Daddy manned two fishing poles that afternoon, a little irritated that my friend Keri had caught the biggest and most fish so far. My sister kept a strict eye on her daughter, Addie, who was a toddler at the time. The child insisted on pestering a pair of stunning black-and-white geese that had decided to live near our pond for the spring. We named them Sonny and Cher. My niece called them "quack quacks," and one of her favorite pastimes was to chase after them in hopes of wrapping her chubby little hands around their necks for a quick hug. Sonny and Cher did not care for Addison, and they often became a bit territorial when she was around.

Disappointed that I hadn't caught anything significant and having reached the point of serenading the fish with my favorite tunes from the *Annie* catalog, I noticed my cork had jerked under the murky water. This was not a nibble, dear reader. This was the big one.

I began to reel. And reel. And reel. The blunt end of the fishing pole was shoved into my gut as I tried to get a better grip on what could only be a double-digit monster. I called for my dad, but he didn't hear me (or chose not to respond).

Unable to turn the dial anymore, I worried that my line was going to snap. Should I swallow my pride and ask for help with the hope that this ten-pound fish would be mine, therefore bestowing bragging rights on me that could be used to my distinct advantage for years and years to come? Or should I risk the chance that this whale of a fish will beat me in a battle of the wills?

I asked Daddy for help. Nature would not reign over me today.

He came over and inspected the fishing pole, and then he, too, struggled. My big strong daddy had a hard time turning the dial. At this point, I started panicking. I would not lose this eleven-pound fish. It would be mine!

I took matters into my own hands, grabbed the line, and began pulling it up the bank. The fish was spinning. My hands were slipping. Daddy was reeling. One more heave, and this twelve-pound beauty slid through the mud and the muck and the goose droppings and the grass.

As we lifted the thirteen-pound catfish, mass chaos ensued. I yelled at my sister to go get a camera. She started on foot, decided to take a golf cart, and proceeded to leave her daughter in her family's care. A goose honked.

My dad, on the other hand, started yelling for Bob at the top of his lungs. That's our neighbor. Still holding my fish, he instructed me to drive him in the other golf cart up to Bob's house, so he could see the fourteen-pounder. Addison was left in the capable hands of Keri. A goose honked.

As I drove like a maniac away from the pond, Jamie drove like a maniac toward the pond, with my mother hanging on for dear life, false eyelashes blowing in the breeze.

Bob showed the appropriate enthusiasm for a fish of this magnitude, and I headed back down to the water's edge for my glamorous photo shoot. When we pulled up, Keri was kneeling beside Addison, proudly holding a tiny little perch.

Wait. What?

Apparently, when all of Addison's blood relatives scattered in golf carts, she decided to entice Sonny and Cher with her two-year-old ways. Fortunately, Keri was there to stop the goose massacre and distracted Addison by allowing her to reel in her line. Lo and behold, a tiny fish was on the other end.

My dad could not contain himself. He jumped out of the golf cart before it had come to a complete stop and somehow lost his shorts, mooning everyone. He and my mother praised Addison for being a proficient angler, Keri laughed her head off, Bob wandered down to see what the commotion was about, my sister took eighty-seven pictures of Addison's fish, and I stood there with a whopping fifteen-pound catfish and no one cared. A goose honked.

That's the power Addison has over our entire family. She is my everything. She always has been.

One day my sister called me and said, "What is the most shocking thing I could tell you right now?" I immediately knew she was pregnant. I was going to be an aunt.

Aunts are like younger, cooler grandparents. I get to spoil the kid rotten whenever I want and send her back to her parents when she's wigging out from having ingested sugar I introduced to her through various candy selections or ice cream flavors or sweet caffeinated beverages.

I'm the one she wants to spend the night with and tell secrets to. I'm the one who has no problem discussing the American Girl Doll catalog or agonizing over the proper size of a hair bow. We talk Harry Potter and guess which house we would have lived in at Hogwarts. We visit Disney World attractions on YouTube and paint each other's nails. I have a nickname I love and drawings I treasure.

When I see her interact with Daddy, I commend her for her patience. She has a special relationship with Mama, and she adores her parents. I love how she nurtures her dolls and cares for her pug. I see a lot of myself in her, which feels odd, because I didn't birth the child.

I often wonder if she's sad that she doesn't have cousins, and I secretly blame myself that she's the lone kid at holiday gatherings. I used to think about the future with tons of grandchildren running around my parents' house. I can see my sister and me lounging around the back porch, barking at whichever child is closest to go and get us a drink. We make it a fun game by timing the little darling to see how fast he can fetch the beverage, hopeful that he can beat the best time clocked by his brother just days before. Jamie nods her head, tickled that I've finally found people younger than me to manipulate.

But this is not our reality. It's just me and my sister's kid. And our future is just as bright.

Addison, I promise you can always come to me when you're angry with your parents, who just don't understand. I promise I will always be there for you when you need to talk, wallow, scream, or laugh. I will celebrate victories and help you through the defeats that will certainly come. I will do my best to be a role model who encourages truth, kindness, and courage. I will never stop praying that you'll know Jesus on a personal level, and I can't wait to see you grow in your faith.

And most importantly, I will always have gum. Both minty and bubble flavors.

22

Texas Forever

For those who stand strong for LOVE
when the storms arrive

When I moved to Houston in 2005, I was intimidated just by driving around in the fourth largest city in America. When people asked me if I loved living here, I would smile politely and change the subject.

I landed in Houston out of necessity. After my divorce, I left the familiarity of Dallas and the convenience of being only two hours away from my family in Hallsville. I was in the public relations world, and I needed to work in a big city. Houston held dear friends who would help me through the hardest time of my life.

But it never really felt like home.

That disconnected feeling shifted in August 2017 when Hurricane Harvey pummeled Houston. I want you to know that what many of you saw reported on the news was not sensationalized. We experienced waves of suffering over the course of many days, some worse than others.

With all the destruction and chaos, two huge blessings helped me lift my hands in thankful praise. Cell towers weren't affected, and most of the city didn't lose power. If I hadn't known what was going on, or if I had been unable to communicate with loved ones and dear friends, I might have cracked.

I almost did.

A new hurricane term I quickly memorized was "the band." These were the tail-like lines of skinny weather occurrences that were constantly slamming into Houston and other surrounding areas, like Missouri City and Katy and Beaumont. The yellow and red ones on the weather map were particularly nasty.

The problem was the bands refused to go away. The eye of Harvey sat over our friends in Victoria, Rockwell, and Corpus Christi (which received the brunt of the actual hurricane), and its bands continued to dump rain on Houston and its surrounding cities.

It happened at least every hour.

It lasted for at least thirty minutes.

Tornadoes often teamed up with the bands.

At first we braced in preparation for the bands. When this had been going on for two entire days without relief, however, I began to shudder at the sight of the bands sweeping across my city, my region, and the entire lower half of my state.

Ridiculous thoughts like *I will never buy this band's T-shirt* rapidly morphed into *Please, Jesus. Make it stop.*

I was thankful for each first responder, police officer, firefighter, member of the coast guard, and the military unit and our local news teams for being on the front lines. We stayed glued to our television sets and phones, praying for that elderly man, that very small baby, that pregnant lady, that child with special needs. I praised the Lord when these individuals were rescued.

Then I grieved with them as reality sat in. They exited one dire situation for another. They had nowhere to go. Not only was their house underwater, but a Walmart sack held the entirety of the belongings they still had. One minute they were safe. The next they realized they were stuck on top of a bridge, waiting for another rescue.

Hundreds of thousands of other people were doing the exact same thing.

This was when my nerves started to frazzle. Reports from friends started pouring in. People posted on Facebook, trying to help steer individuals with boats to their loved ones.

Yes. *Boats.*

Every single major road and feeder was underwater. Every. Single. One. That is not an exaggeration. Because the bands had been playing constantly for forty-eight-hours, relief couldn't reach us. It couldn't get down the street.

At some point, this quote from Mister Rogers flooded my memory: "When I was a boy and I would see scary things in the news, my mother would say to me, 'Look for the helpers. You will always find people who are helping.'"*

I clung to that side of hope, because my heart couldn't take any more devastation. People who hadn't been hit as hard came out in droves. They mobilized.

Where did they come from? They came from down the street. They drove in from San Antonio. Their trucks pulled boats. A convoy of fishermen from Louisiana made their way across their state into ours. Even though they were dealing with their own bands, they headed west. They drove right into the line of fire. Perfect strangers became lifesavers. Back and forth. Into the neighborhood and out. Countless times. More people. More pets. More relief. More devastation.

We are a city that floods. We've weathered storms before, so we have practices in place for when bayous fill and roads overflow.

---

* Fred Rogers, *The Mister Rogers Parenting Book* (Philadelphia: Running Press, 2002), 107.

Specific emergency locations are prepared for droves of people when they're in need. This is not our first rodeo.

Unfortunately, displaced people couldn't get to our prepared shelters because Interstate 10 was literally under water. So was downtown. And neighborhoods in Meyerland and parts of Friendswood. The entire region was fighting the flood.

We sat and watched the helpers on TV and online. They broke into an elementary school and set up shop. Even with no food and no running water, people were dropping off blankets, diapers, and cans of gasoline for the boats. They shared rations. They shared umbrellas. They gave the raincoats off their own backs to shield others.

We watched the helpers. We watched as they worked in the constant downpour of rain.

Soon the guilt set in.

We learned a family in need was without power. Texts flurried back and forth. Abled bodies began begging the Lord to restore that family's power and take their own. Strong wills asked the Lord to flood their own home, so another home could be spared. Friends helped set up makeshift shelters in neighborhoods, because they were in the neighborhoods hit the worst.

That's a different level of "helper."

Eventually the news and social media became too much. I had to shut them down. I had to walk away. I had to accept the fact that I was landlocked and I could quite literally do nothing as the texts and messages continued to blow up my phone:

The water is at the driveway.

Now the water is at the front door.

Pray.

We're moving everything onto the kitchen counters.

We're sweeping out water.

Pray the rain stops.

It's coming too fast.

Please pray!

We're evacuating to one of those makeshift shelters.
Pray for us.

I hit my knees on the floor and cried out to the Lord to please
. . . make . . . the . . . rain . . . stop.

When the rain didn't stop, bitterness sat in, because I was
a good person who hadn't done anything wrong, and all I had
asked was for the Lord to stop the flood. *You made the rain, for
heaven's sake. Just stop the rain.*

When it didn't stop, fear crept in.

My roommate, Lara, calmed me down by encouraging me to
look at the facts: We had shelter, we had power, and water was
not at our front door, at least not yet. We had prepared for the
worst. We would be fine.

That helped. Because we would be fine. We would.

My friend Stephanie, who worked four days in a row at the
children's hospital, checked in. Even though she was taking care
of sick babies and worried parents, I was selfish and texted an
admission that I felt helpless.

When a heart-wrenching text came in from a friend who was
in desperate need for the rains to stop, I straight-up hit the panic
button and phoned another friend after midnight.

In a raw, completely self-centered moment, I forgot about
everyone else suffering and told Jill I was in bad shape. She
launched into prayer. And she spoke truth.

It's hard to see and recognize a good and loving Father when
you're surrounded by heartbreak. It's difficult to lean into His everlasting arms when all you've done for three days is desperately pray
for the rains to stop, but they don't. It's annoying to be told *this
too shall pass* when you're sitting right in the middle of it, unable
to help in any way. Not to mention the fact that it's not passing.

But Jill spoke truth.

She reminded me that our God is not a God of fear. He's a God
who loves us deeply, even though for whatever reason, we and
the rest of our city and region were experiencing something we

never wanted to experience again. The fear and anxiety didn't come from Him.

We were being attacked. And not just with flood levels. We were being attacked spiritually.

Pulling Scripture from my brain, I began reminding myself that God is a victorious warrior (Zeph. 3:17). That I have hope because His compassions never fail and they're new every morning (Lam. 3:21–23).

He is sovereign. And He is good. He made sure 365 verses in the Bible teach us to guard against fear and anxiety. One verse for every day. That tells me fear and anxiety will creep up often and that we need multiple verses to combat the attack.

Second Timothy 1:7 says, "For the Spirit God gave us does not make us timid, but gives us power, love and self-discipline."

He created the heavens and the earth. He created me too. I am my Beloved's and He is mine.

I sat and watched the dawn break. I couldn't help people in and out of boats in the pouring rain. I couldn't comfort women at a shelter. I couldn't take nine-one-one calls or make sure children were safe in their beds at the hospital.

Days later, the rain finally stopped, and those of us who could drive to the church began to mobilize. We were a skeleton crew, but we were mighty. Plans were put into place. A command center was organized. Slowly, the calls came in letting us know which families from our church had been hit. I stopped counting when we reached thirty.

A Harvey page on our church website was built in a matter of hours. People signed up in droves to work, provide equipment, offer housing, and care for misplaced pets. We had boats, trucks, trailers, dehumidifiers, power tools, wheelbarrows, and willing bodies who had evacuated the city waiting on standby, waiting for roads to clear.

I was deemed the field supply coordinator, or field czar in some circles. If our teams out on the job needed something, they called me, and I got it to them. If they wanted something, I found it and got it to them. We had one problem, though: most of the supplies we needed were in stores like Home Depot or Lowe's. Unfortunately, half of those stores were under water or on the other side of water. Or they were sold out of everything.

We hit the ground running the moment the waters receded and the major highways opened enough to safely navigate them. On the first day we officially began our Harvey cleanup campaign, one thousand people showed up to help. I had two hammers, one wheelbarrow, a few brooms, and some leather gloves.

My daddy was right. Sometimes all you need is grit and determination to get a job done.

The helpers showed up every morning, grabbed the few tools we'd collected, and headed out to assist people in need. Around noon, the half-day shift arrived. Later the helpers all returned with sore backs, blistered fingers, tired eyes, and a humbled look that screamed *Well done, my good and faithful servant.*

When you think about hurricane recovery, demolition and cleanup probably come to mind. This is the bulk of the work, and the strong can be found here. But other pockets of recovery often go unnoticed. These are the people who cook countless meals for families and helpers. They do laundry and babysit small children. They drop off gift cards and donate various contents from their own homes.

These helpers console dazed folks who watch as their home is taken apart piece by piece and their ruined belongings are placed in garbage bags to sit in their front yard for who knows how long. They gently tell an older man who picks through a library of soggy books that he won't be able to salvage his precious collection with a hair dryer. They allow a woman to grieve over her spoiled wedding china that has been infected by the mold.

They buy a replacement American Girl Doll for the little one who lost hers in the flood. When she cries, "You found her!"

the parents make eye contact. There's an unspoken agreement to just go with it, believing God will be okay with this tiny white lie.

Yes, baby girl. We found her.

I began to notice the little things that made me happy during my time as field czar. I straight-up shouted "Hallelujah!" when someone brought two wheelbarrows in from out of town. I had the pleasure of explaining to a six-year-old how we were helping the helpers who were helping the people whose houses had flooded as he stared at rows and rows and rows of bleach. I cried when five dehumidifiers showed up.

Praise to the boys who drove four hours from a Dallas junior college to help us. They found us by typing "church, Houston, work crew" into Google. Bless their sweet hearts. And their young muscles. Those sure did come in handy.

One of the biggest gifts came from Alissa and the supporters of Arise Africa. As you know, Alissa is not one to just sit around when there's a call to serve. Who cares that she's in Fort Worth? She had the ever-so-brilliant idea to start an Amazon Wish List and gave her donors a week to meet the need.

Boy, did they meet the need.

Imagine a twenty-foot box truck. Now imagine that truck completely full of everything you could ever need for hurricane recovery. We were overwhelmed by Alissa's tenacity and the generosity of the Arise Africa donors. We were encouraged by the provision and by how many families would be touched by this gift.

We were also nervous about where we were going to unload the big truck full of crowbars, bleach, masks, gloves, snow shovels, brooms, cleaning supplies, and enough Rubbermaid to rival Mama's Christmas decoration containers in the attic.

I casually mentioned to my friend Amy that we needed a warehouse. She texted her boss, Matt, and in less than an hour we had one—air-conditioned, no less.

Once word got out that we had a warehouse, all sorts of opportunities for ministry opened. My friend Crystal arranged for a box truck of donated items of her own to arrive a few days after the Arise Africa truck arrived. We had enough diapers for every baby in town.

It was glorious.

My opinion of the city changed after Harvey. I realized I could take Houston or leave Houston, but what I will never forget is the way friends, families, and strangers were united, as one. I personally saw the hands and feet of Christ. I may be annoyed with traffic by the Galleria and feel like I'm going to melt into the ground come June, but I will always love my fellow Houstonians.

It's a deep love that comes from sacrifice and service.

Stephanie said it best with this text: "We are thankful that thousands of years ago, God poured out something stronger than flood waters. He covered us with the shed blood of Jesus Christ and commissioned us to, above all else, love our neighbors well."

Harvey was a softball pitch for us to practice this command. We took this time of heartbreak to sharpen those skills. And we're wiser, more compassionate, and fulfilled people as a result.

Especially when three months later, the Astros would win the World Series.

Houston strong. Texas forever.

23

Mary, Did You Know?

For those who LOVE *unconditionally*

One of my favorite people in the Bible is Jesus's mother, Mary. I like her because she's an inspiration to me. At such a young age, she processed some rather big news with an attitude of trust and faith, and then she faced a multitude of unexpected situations with grace.

Let me be clear. I don't necessarily relate to Mary in her specific circumstances. I could never have done what she did. In the Gospel of Luke, the angel Gabriel visits Mary to tell her she's going to have a baby. I imagine Mary thinking all sorts of things and feeling all the feels. But after she considers the news, she has just one question: "How will this be . . . since I am a virgin?" (Luke 1:34).

I think she believes Gabriel; she's just asking a biological question. She doesn't doubt the promise; she just doesn't understand the process. Gabriel is quick to fill in the blanks. He tells her, "The Holy Spirit," and then, "Nothing will be impossible with

God" (vv. 35 and 37 ESV). Mary's response is convicting. She looks up and says, "I am the servant of the Lord; let it be to me according to your word" (v. 38).

Had I been in Mary's sandals, this event would have gone a little differently:

Gabriel: "Mary! You're pregnant! By the Holy Spirit! You will call Him Jesus! Congratulations, girl!"

My First Reaction—Denial

Oh Gabe, dude, I know you're God's messenger, and that in and of itself is so cool, but I'm definitely not your girl. I think you took a wrong turn at the Sea of Galilee, because there isn't any way this is going to happen.

Also, a ton of girls named Mary live around here. It's like what the name Jennifer will be in the 1980s. Are you sure you aren't confusing me for one of them? I hear Magdalene is a hoot. Let me send you her contact information. What's your cell number?

My Second Reaction—Shame

Gabe, what will people say? I'm not married to Joseph yet. Can you come back in eight months when this might make more sense? The women at the well are *not* going to let this go. I can see the tabloids now: "Mary: Good Girl Gone Bad." My mother doesn't want to read that headline, Gabe. No, thank you.

My Third Reaction—Bargaining

Surely someone else can do the job better than me, right? I know! My cousin Elizabeth. She's already pregnant. Let's stick this one in with hers. They can be womb mates! That will work.

My Fourth Reaction—Bitterness

Really, Gabe? You're not going to let me get pregnant traditionally?

Fast-forward a few months, and Mary is indeed with child. Right around the time she's about to give birth, Caesar Augustus issues a decree for a census to be taken of the entire Roman world, and everyone must register. Since Joseph belongs to the house of David, he has to go to Bethlehem. He borrows a donkey and tells his very pregnant wife that she needs to hop on for the four-day trek.

My Fifth Reaction—Anger

You have *got* to be kidding me! Seriously? This is soooooooo my life. *Of course* Caesar Augustus issued a decree for a census when I'm nine hundred months pregnant. Nothing ever goes my way. And, Joe, could you not have scored a chariot from one of your buddies? A donkey? *Really?* I insist you call Gabe on his cell phone. Isn't that a benefit of knowing an angel? Having him on speed dial for situations like this? Can someone get me one of those donut pillows over here, please? And maybe an iPad to distract me from how sucky my life is right now? I'm going to need a Wi-Fi hot spot, because if anything calls for all seven seasons of *Gilmore Girls*, it's this moment right here.

Mary and Joseph finally made it to Bethlehem, and she went into labor. Scripture tells us there was no room at the inn. Whether she was turned away by a business owner or by Joseph's family is debatable. What we do know is she gave birth in a barn or a cave. She probably looked at her humble surroundings and thought, *I did not expect this. However, in Him all things are possible. Let's do this.*

Once again, this event would have been a little different with me.

My First Reaction—Fear

No. No, no, no, no, *no*. This is not in my birth plan. Does this piece of parchment say anything about cattle lowing? I don't think so. I need drugs, and I need them now.

After the fear set in and I knew this was happening, I would probably try another tactic.

My Second Reaction—Control Freak

Is this area sterilized yet? Let's rip sheets and boil water. Someone needs to stop that kid from drumming over there, because the first sounds my baby hears need to be soothing tones, not a wicked backbeat.

One more thing. This guy named Herod is going to be chasing after us, so someone should scout a place for us to live. Make it far enough away to be safe, but close enough so my parents can babysit. It must be in a really good school district, because in case you aren't clued in yet, *this is the Messiah*. The neighborhood needs to be close to a Trader Joe's and an Orangetheory. Make it happen, people.

Sometimes, we must expect the unexpected, and deal with it. Because God's plans will always be fulfilled.

God had big plans for Mary. She was a nobody from a nothing town in the middle of nowhere. And Scripture tells us she was favored. Not because of what she had done, but because of what God was about to do through her.

Society was expecting a Savior of royal birth. They were looking for the King of Kings, the Prince of Peace. What they got was a child born a lowly birth.

Talk about unexpected.

We have the benefit of knowing the rest of the story. We know that thirty-three years later, Mary watched Jesus take on the sins of the world and die a cruel death on the cross.

I can't even begin to imagine what my reaction would have been.

But because of that ultimate sacrifice for us, we should remember how Mary trusted, how she obeyed, how she held steadfast to her faith, and how she loved. Her words are just as powerful today as they were so many years ago: "I am the servant of the Lord; let it be to me according to your word" (Luke 1:38 ESV).

We know the end of the story. We can choose to trust our sovereign God and His path for us. Expect the unexpected. For in Him, all things are possible. For in Him, we are loved.

Conclusion

For those of us who long for LOVE

Let me ask you a few questions:

- Why do you think a stack of romantic comedy DVDs from my shelf and a directory of fake boyfriends are featured in this book?
- How many of you have seeing Celine Dion in person on your musical bucket list so you can hear "My Heart Will Go On" the way the good Lord intended, which is at The Colosseum at Caesars Palace in Las Vegas?
- Do you think it's just wrong that I have the dialogue of *Sleeping Beauty* memorized?
- Do you believe the love triangle we see in nearly every Hallmark movie story line is a coincidence?

If I look closely at my life and dissect the pieces that bring me the most joy, it's evident that rooting for the love story comes naturally to me. It just manifests itself in several different ways.

Love is being seen and liked for who I am. So I dance. I speak. I write.

Love is being desired. It's why I still get butterflies (and hives) when I think about my first kiss and the euphoria of dating. It's also the reason I try to convince myself at least once a month that I should bite the bullet and join an online dating service.

Love is never wanting anyone else to feel invisible or undesirable. That's why I volunteer at Houston's WorkFaith Connection. Or I get on an airplane and serve lunch to kids in Zambia or speak to a bunch of students in Cuba.

If love is all around me, interpreted in many ways, why do I often feel like something is missing? Do you ever get the feeling there has to be more to life than what you're currently experiencing? Do you ever sit at your kitchen table and wonder, *This can't be it, can it?*

I do.

The desire to locate this missing piece of my life slowly infiltrates my subconscious. I wrote an entire book about how I try to fill that void by working longer hours or expanding my bank account. I focus on my status, my busy schedule, and my approval addiction. I live my best life through my Instagram account. I become obsessed with getting married, getting pregnant, getting praise, getting ahead, or getting even.

Yet no amount of power ballads, holiday love stories, salsa classes, mission trips, fake relationships, or trips to Disney World sustains that best-life feeling. Dreaming about my future husband, spending time with my family and friends, serving with my church community, or escaping into pop culture doesn't do the trick either. And even if Chris Pine did choose to answer my fan mail, my guess is that the euphoria would last only days before I felt that familiar void again.

So here I am, back at square one. Why is it I feel as if a fracture in my emotional makeup needs to be mended?

The fact is we are not complete. Our need to feel loved is ingrained in our souls. It's been that way since the beginning.

In the book of Genesis is a lovely story about Adam and Eve living in Paradise with God. Everything is wonderful and peaceful, with only one rule: do not eat from the Tree of Knowledge of Good and Evil.

Eve was tempted, she ate the fruit, and *boom!* Sin enters the world on page 2 of my Bible. We have barely started the story when Adam and Eve's relationship with the Lord shifts, and they're banned from the Garden.

From that moment on, we were parted from God, unworthy to be in His presence thanks to our sinful nature. As a result, we will never feel fully satisfied on this earth.

Here's the kicker, though. This was God's plan all along. He wanted to show the quintessential act of love. So He sacrificed His Son.

This is the ultimate love story.

Over the course of more than two thousand years, the forty narrators of the Bible have pointed to Jesus as the way, the truth, and the life. We needed to be separated from God to understand our need for a Savior. We needed that space to rely completely on Him in faith, hope, and love.

Until we reunite with our Maker face-to-face, we'll settle for substitutes to satiate our longing. Romantic movies and poetic story lines will fill us with faith. Gorgeous lyrics will fill our ears with hope. And intentional relationships with our families and friends will fill our hearts with love.

And now these three remain: faith, hope and love. But the greatest of these is love. (1 Corinthians 13:13)

Acknowledgments

Of all the mixed tapes I've painstakingly produced in the last four decades, this one is by far my greatest creation. I admit that at first glance, the song selections may seem weird, but I've included my train of thought that led me to these stellar choices. I fully believe this omission of information is where I dropped the ball with physical therapist William. I will not let that happen again.

Caroline Applegate — "How Deep Is Your Love" by the Bee-Gees. Sweet Caroline, not only is your love deep, but it is equally wide. And I think you will be the only one on this list who appreciates the vocal stylings and fashion sense of the Bee Gees.

Susan Barrett — "I Love to Laugh" from *Mary Poppins*. It's true. I do love to laugh. And any time I'm near you, I know I will be laughing. And probably snorting. And choking on candy corn. But it will be worth it.

Pam Boehm — "When You Love Someone" by Bryan Adams. This book would not exist without your kitchen table and back porch. Thank you for leaving me a key to your house so I could pretend to be a serious writer in a log cabin in the woods. You mean the world to me.

Kristin Cameron — "I and Love and You" by The Avett Brothers. Straight to the point. Just like you.

Lindsay Chernosky — "Love Is an Open Door" from *Frozen*. This one is random, but don't feel bad, Lindsay. It spoke to me. Because you have a key to the back door of my website and I will forever be grateful for all you do to make IHGB an actual running machine.

Emmarie Clark — "Let Your Love Flow" by Bellamy Brothers. You love people well, Emmarie Clark. Never forget that.

Amy Cooper — "Lover of the Light" by Mumford and Sons. As you are the friend who experienced with me one of the quintessential live musical events of my life, I trust you will be ready to secure future Mumford and Sons tickets should they ever grace Houston with their presence again. I can't handle the pressure.

Ann Corrigan — "Young Love" by The Judds. Ann, you know what's coming. You should have gone to their concert with us. I don't mean to bring up your greatest regret of 2013, but I feel it's important to remind you to never let another concert go by when your friends tell you to build a bridge between your heart and The Judds.

Alex Eisenhuth — "Love Will Turn You Around" by Kenny Rogers. Whenever you feel turned around, you can always come home!

Gary Eisenhuth — "I Love Rock and Roll" by Joan Jett and the Blackhearts. I'm sorry I can't feature you on my podcast because normal people will have never heard of your favorite rock bands. I still love you though!

Keri Engle — "When I Fall in Love" by Michael Bublé. Oh, Keri, thank you for introducing me to Mr. Bublé so many years ago. And thank you for picking me up off the ground in the parking lot when I tripped before his concert and fell on my face. It's a good thing that older lady was there to lend me a Kleenex from her purse to stop the bleeding.

Emily Fraker — "On the Wings of Love" by Jeffrey Osborne. There aren't enough words to thank the person who allows a gaggle of crazy girls to infiltrate her home every Monday night to watch *The Bachelor*. Thank you for having such fluffy couch cushions I can hide behind!

Jill Hatley — "I Just Called to Say I Love You" by Stevie Wonder. Rest assured I'll say it as Kristen Wiig in her Target Lady voice.

Connie Haugneland — "Can You Feel the Love Tonight" from *The Lion King*. Even though this song gives me hives, and is the absolute worst, I knew I had to pick a Disney classic for you.

Stephanie Holstead — "Season of Love" from *Rent*. It feels like I've known you for five hundred twenty-five thousand six hundred years. Thank you for being the friend who has a Broadway playlist on her iTunes.

Autumn Hugo — "I Like It, I Love It" by Tim McGraw. Your enthusiasm for life is infectious. Never change.

Lisa Jackson — "Have I Told You Lately" by Rod Stewart. I know I've told you lately what annoys me and what confuses me and what makes me want to smash my head into a brick wall. Please know that you are so dear to me and really good at talking people off ledges!

Catha Jaynes — "Your Love Never Fails" by Jesus Culture. I know I can count on you for anything. Because you are with me always.

Stephanie Johnson — "Love in Any Language" by Sandi Patty. Could this acknowledgement be any more perfect for you, Steph?

Shannon Joiner — " L-O-V-E" by Nat King Cole. Did I pick this because you are a really good speller? Not quite. It reminded me of all the times you kicked butt at Instagram during my first book launch. I will always be in awe of your social media skills. And your ability to rock a hair braid.

Rebecca Juillerat — "Love Will Keep Us Together" by Captain & Tennille. Love will keep us together. So will queso. And our obsession with *Gilmore Girls*.

Terri Langford — "Carrying Your Love with Me" by George Strait. Don't get me started on YOU MOVING AWAY FROM ME! I understand that I'm projecting that you will be carrying your love for me in this instance. It seems on brand for you, so I'm going to stick with it.

Anne Letzerich — "Vision of Love" by Mariah Carey. For the woman who makes the world beautiful, this one's for you, Anne.

Nancy Jane McMillan — "Greatest Love of All" by Whitney Houston. Not only did we traipse around Israel, barely escaping jail time, but I will remember you singing "Ave Maria" in the Church of Saint Anne. If anyone can handle Whitney, it's you, Cone.

Julie Medford — "The Power of Love" by Celine Dion. Thank you for helping me pick out so many outfits in high school. I'm sure your carefully chosen ensemble paired with my killer dance moves is what made Miles lean in for the kiss. I'm forever in your debt.

Paula Meyers — "Crazy Love" by Van Morrison. We're just two crazy kids who love to play cards and memorize Scripture together. I'm sorry there's not a song called "Nerd Love."

Sarah Nash — "Glory of Love" by Bette Midler. You have one of the biggest hearts I know. And it's glorious.

Dennis and Danielle Postiglione — "Lookin' For Love" by Johnny Lee. I know I should call y'all Bud and Sissy, but "HEY TATOO" and "UNCLE BOB" are fighting for a place on this page. *Urban Cowboy* forever!

Lara Pringle — "Love Story" by Taylor Swift. Thank you for letting me live with you and being the brains behind the title of this book. I think you are so sweet to assume T. Swift is going to spy it in a Barnes & Noble and tweet about it to her bajillion fans. When I become rich and famous after that happens, I want you to know I'm not moving out.

Linda Pringle — "How Sweet It Is (To Be Loved by You)" by James Taylor. I am your biggest fan!

Todd Richards — "Love Man" by Otis Redding. To the dude we all call to save the day, I salute you, Todd Richards!

Krystal Scott — "Who Loves You" by Frankie Valli and The Four Seasons. Who has two thumbs and adores Krystal Scott? THIS GIRL!

Audrey Shaak — "International Love" by Pitbull. Okay, so I wanted to pick something that signified you gallivanting all over the world at the drop of a hat. Also, Pitbull had to be featured somewhere in this book. You're amazing, Audrey!

Melanie Shankle — "As Long as You Love Me" by Backstreet Boys. As the song says, "I don't care who you are, where you're from, what you did, as long as you love me." Sincerely, Lincee, president of the Melanie Shankle Fan Club.

Kristie Shankles — "Love Ran Red" by Chris Tomlin. It's Tomlin. Duh.

Angel Texada — "And I Love Her" by Harry Connick Jr. Not only is Harry from NOLA, but you played a significant role in two very important chapters of this book. It meant the world to me and I love you for it.

Natalie Weakly — "Elephant Love Medley" from Moulin Rouge. To the woman who can belt out this entire medley and still keep perfect pitch as I "harmonize" beside you on the way home from a Lionel Richie concert, thank you for putting up with me all these years.

Ranelle Woolrich — "Love Like No Other" by Point of Grace. I said it last time and I'll say it again: everyone needs a Ranelle in his or her life.

Revell Team — "Crazy Little Thing Called Love" by Queen. I know you labeled my folder with a crazy tab, but we made it to the end! Thank y'all for everything.

IHGB Readers — "Endless Love" by Lionel Richie and Diana Ross. None of this would be possible without the folks who read iHateGreenBeans. I have no words for what your support means to me. My cup runneth over.

Addison — "I Will Always Love You" by Dolly Parton. You are my everything and I love you. Thank you for letting me be your Slink.

Jamie Eisenhuth — "(Love Will) Turn Back the Hands of Time" from *Grease 2*. Stop laughing. This song is perfect for you and you know it! Ten bucks says you secretly watched your hidden copy of *Grease 2* just a few weeks ago. I know because I did the same thing. Michael is so dreamy in his silver motorcycle suit.

Mummy — "Island of Love" by Elvis Presley. The King had a lot of songs with *love* in the title, but I know this one has to be your favorite. *Aloha from Hawaii* is your most worn-out vinyl record, next to *The Sound of Music* and the Muppets Christmas album. We are an eclectic family and I'm glad we embrace it.

Daddy — "Papa Loved Mama" by Garth Brooks. Thank you for being the strong rock of our little family. I love you, Daddy!

Jesus — "I Love You Lord" by Hillsong. Once again, it's all about *You*, Jesus. With the hope that You will be glorified, I surrender these pages.

"We love because he first loved us" (1 John 4:19).

Sources

Ardolino, Emile, dir. *Dirty Dancing*; Santa Monica, CA: Lionsgate, 1987. DVD.

Crane, David, Marta Kauffman. *Friends*. Season 5, episode 14, "The One Where Everybody Finds Out." Aired February 11, 1999, on NBC.

Heckerling, Amy, dir. *Clueless*; Hollywood, CA: Paramount Pictures, 1995. DVD.

Hogan, P. J., dir. *My Best Friend's Wedding*; Culver City, CA: TriStar Pictures, 1997. DVD.

Jackson, Mick, dir. *The Bodyguard*; Burbank, CA: Warner Bros., 1992. DVD.

Marshall, Garry, dir. *Beaches*; Burbank, CA: Buena Vista Pictures, 1988. DVD.

Metter, Alan, dir. *Girls Just Want to Have Fun*; Atlanta, GA: New World Pictures, 1985.

Meyers, Nancy, dir. *The Holiday*; Culver City, CA: Columbia Pictures Corporation, 2006. DVD.

Turteltaub, Jon, dir. *While You Were Sleeping*; Burbank, CA: Hollywood Pictures, 1997. DVD.

Weir, Peter, dir. *Dead Poets Society*; Burbank, CA: Buena Vista Pictures Distribution, 1998. DVD.

Lincee Ray is the author of *Why I Hate Green Beans* and an accidental blogging superstar who writes for *Entertainment Weekly* and the Associated Press. An active speaker, she can be found at her popular website www.iHateGreenBeans.com, where she makes it clear that she believes it's important to tell your story—even if it makes you seem a little crazy. She lives in Texas.

Connect with Lincee!

For more on Lincee's blog, podcast, and speaking schedule, visit **iHateGreenBeans.com**.

 LinceeRay   @LinceeRay   @Lincee

"**Lincee Ray is funny.** Really funny. By the end of this book, you'll think of Lincee as a favorite friend: someone who shoots straight, finds the funny in every situation, and reminds you what matters most. **You are in for a treat!**"

—SOPHIE HUDSON, author of *Giddy Up, Eunice* and cohost of *The Big Boo Cast* podcast